The Twelve
Taking up the Mantle of Christ

Taking up the Mantle of Christ

Tim R. Barker, D. Min.

Superintendent of the South Texas District of the Assemblies of God

THE TWELVE: TAKING UP THE MANTLE OF CHRIST,
Barker, Tim.

1st ed.

Scripture passages are from The Holy Bible, New International Version® (NIV®), copyright © 1973, 1978, 1984, 2011 by Biblica, Inc.™ All rights reserved. Used by permission of Zondervan.

This book and its contents are wholly the creation and intellectual property of Tim Barker.

This book may not be reproduced in whole or in part, by electronic process or any other means, without written permission of the author.

ISBN: 978-1-7358529-2-8

Copyright © 2021 by Tim Barker

All Rights Reserved

Dedication

To my TIMOTHY PROJECT GROUP,
young leaders with whom I have the privilege of meeting monthly. During our time together, we strategize and GROW TOGETHER in the LORD.

Table of Contents

Peter	1
Andrew	10
James	22
Philip	36
Simon	46
Matthew	59
Thomas	71
Jude	84
James the Less	94
Nathaniel	104
John	116
Judas	126

About Tim R. Barker 139

A Final Word 141

Peter

When you think about the apostles, you probably have in your mind a picture of great men of God who healed the sick, raised the dead, did great miracles everywhere they went, and exercised faith that was unshakable and perfect – and if you do, you are not thinking about the twelve apostles that followed Jesus!

The kind of men that became Jesus' right-hand men were very much like you and me. Jesus hand-picked them, and they were quite a motley crew! Studying them will help us appreciate the love God has in picking us to be His followers ... we have many of the same weaknesses that these so called "giants" of the faith did, and some of their strengths also! Charles Spurgeon, the Great Preacher, once said, "It is a good thing that God chose me before I was born, because He surely would not have afterwards."

If you think that you have problems with doubts, or struggle with being obedient, you are in good company ... not only with Christians sitting around you right now but also those who walked with Jesus in His own day!

While Peter was quite impetuous, God saw the potential of the man who would one day be capable of leading His church and becoming a steady man of God; weaknesses on our part do not disqualify us from being loved by God and used by Him ... we have hope!

Peter had this thing for "jumping into things" – or "jumping" before looking! His nature was to immediately respond to emotional stirrings! This was a "double-edged sword" quality; if the right thing came along, he was quick to commit to it; however, around the wrong event or the wrong crowd, he could just as easily commit to it or them! This made Peter's life quite interesting. Sometimes you loved this guy and at other times you wanted to clobber him! Like the time Peter JUMPED overboard to walk on the water to Jesus – no thought about what he did until he was on the water and then saw the waves. Taking his eyes off Jesus, he began to sink! This describes a lot of Christians! After a stirring sermon, they are ready to make a commitment. It is the follow-through that becomes the problem, especially when they see the stormy seas around them!

When the women told Peter and the others that Jesus was alive, he JUMPED UP and ran to the tomb to see for himself – a quick start, just not a good marathon runner yet! Luke 24:12 says, "Peter, however, got up and ran to the tomb. Bending over, he saw the strips of linen lying by themselves, and he went away, wondering to himself what had happened." When Peter realized it was Jesus on the shore he JUMPED into the water and swam to shore to be with Him!

Peter is likeable; you can't help but love a guy who is this motivated. Jesus saw potential, and impetuous people have potential! Focusing or channeling their emotions is all they need, and to help them learn to think before they jump! There are those shining moments, however, when Peter is moved to jump for the right thing, such as his commitment to Christ!

Though many others stopped following Christ when they realized how hard the commitment was going to be, Peter didn't flinch, at least not on this occasion! People who have strong emotions can be strongly committed, at least until some other strong emotion comes along that pulls them aside or to something else. Peter later would deny Jesus when he was extremely fearful and disillusioned. Once, however, those fears were relieved by Jesus' appearance, he came back!

Impetuous disciples are very motivated people. They are quick to move on something, although they may not have thought through all the dynamics. Peter was a great Pentecostal! Perhaps this is why he typified the whole group on the day of Pentecost; he becomes the first spokesman and leader of the new Pentecostal church! Later he is confronted by Paul for reacting emotionally with some Gentiles. When his Jewish brethren show up, he acts like a hypocrite and Paul calls him down on it publicly. Peter was emotional! It is interesting to note, however, that this was not viewed by God as a negative trait; Jesus picked Peter to be the leader of the group! Emotions are good – they just need discipline!

Give me "jump first" Christians over "never move" ones any day! It is easier to steer a ship than to push one! Ecclesiastes 9:4 says, "A live dog is better than a dead lion." Impetuous people tend to feel guilty and insecure because of their nature, yet these are people that God desires and is willing to shape – power under control!

Impetuous people can be sensitive to fear. This is what at times makes them "jumpy." Peter often did crazy things when he was afraid! Fear is an emotion ... which is a part of a "Peter" personality. When Peter first saw Jesus walking on the water he cried out in great fear thinking Jesus was a ghost. Then when he knew it wasn't, he jumped off the boat and started walking toward Jesus until, of course, he started sinking because of fear of the waves. Then Jesus rescued him! "Peter" people can be fearful people; they may lean towards "worry" at times. Peter was afraid when God spoke from heaven and said how "pleased He was with His son Jesus." Peter fell to the ground in fear. Jesus had to reassure him and tell him to get up. Matthew 17:6 tells us, "When the disciples heard this, they fell facedown to the ground, terrified." There is probably a little bit of a "Peter personality" in everyone.

Peter, when confused, acted strange; in this case he cut off an ear of a servant who was trying to arrest Jesus! During unexpected moments, "Peters" can react with panic. Emotions drive them to act without thinking first! Even when Peter saw Jesus after the resurrection, he was confused and in panic again, thinking, "Jesus is a ghost!" Confusion can come with this personality trait. What is needed is information and calm. Jesus, at this point, offers Peter and the others the chance to touch Him and feel His scars so they would realize this was real, and not be afraid or confused!

Fortunately, Jesus sees much more than just our weaknesses. In fact, it is Peter's weakness – his emotionally strong reactions – that will become his strength once they are focused and disciplined! Peter brings to mind the verse, "When we are weak we are strong."

It is noteworthy that Jesus often picked Peter to be with Him when others were not. When Jesus was transfigured, Peter was there. Of course, he reacted emotionally and told Jesus how they should erect three tents, one for Jesus, one for Moses, and one for Elijah. While Jesus didn't appreciate the offer, Jesus still loved the man! Jesus kept Peter close to Him. This close communion is what Peter needed for the balance in his life! All this close communion would eventually overcome Peter's weaknesses. You can't be around Jesus in such close communion and not have it effect you!

Jesus took Peter, James, and John, His closest friends, with Him into the garden of Gethsemane. Out of those three, Peter seems to be the closest, for when Jesus comes back to find them, it is Peter He speaks to first! Jesus' toughest time was spent in communion with Peter, although Peter slept through it! Jesus' choice would not likely be ours ... but again, He sees what we do not! Peter represents the kind of disciple that Jesus loves, impetuous but loved! There is hope, Saint! If Jesus can take Peter, He might do well with you!

Jesus' confidence in Peter is shown in Luke

22:31-32. Jesus states Satan's desire to sift Peter like wheat – yet Jesus prays for Peter and tells him that when it is all over, after Peter has failed, he will yet "strengthen his brothers." Jesus was confident that Peter would turn back again! Impetuous doesn't mean stupid. Peter might react out of fear and do the wrong thing, but Jesus knew Peter wasn't shallow or dumb; Peter would be a "rock"! Jesus' final commission was in John 21:15-17. Three times Jesus asks Peter if Peter loves Him! Peter is hurt by this three-fold asking, yet this is what Peter needed to get rid of his own pain. After all, he had denied Jesus three times days earlier! After each affirmation, Jesus instructs Peter to "FEED MY SHEEP" or "LAMBS" ... in other words – lead!

Jesus' trust in Peter is revealed at the end. It is to Peter that Jesus gives instructions for pastoral ministry – this emotional guy who often reacted from the emotion of the moment is Christ's choice of leadership! It is true that it took years with Christ to bring discipline to Peter's emotional nature! Jesus' love and guidance for an impetuous man gives hope for all of us who tend to be ruled by our emotions or the events of the moment ... keep your love for

Christ, and when you make a mistake, come back. Jesus loves you more than you can know!

Jesus' final words to Peter in this passage: "FOLLOW ME" ... This is how his nature would stay in check! As he followed Christ, his very weakness would become the passion to do God's work and stay on course! There is yet hope for all of us PENTECOSTAL CHRISTIANS – YOU KNOW, ALL OF US EMOTIONAL CHRISTIANS!

Peter is easy to identify with, like so many of us who go from hot to cold in our walk with God. Often, we are afraid, yet God loves us deeply! Like Peter, our Lord keeps working with us. Peter became a great disciple – and so can you!

Andrew

When the term "GREAT MINISTRY" is used it conjures up many pictures – great teachers, great preachers, Mother Teresa, Billy Graham, John Wesley, Jonathan Edwards, etc. Yet, the vast majority of "GREAT MINISTRY" in God's kingdom has been done by much less well-known saints over the centuries ... the "ANDREWS" of the ages!

Andrew was not an up-front person as much as he was a middleman ... helping to bring together issues and people. He didn't so much teach others by mouth as much as he brought people to Jesus for Jesus to teach them. Andrew was the guy who was looking for bridges or making them ... the church of

Jesus Christ needs "Andrews"!

The great musician Leonard Bernstein was asked once which, in his opinion, is the hardest instrument to play. He replied, "Second fiddle. Everyone wants to play first but few are interested in second." Andrew was much loved by Jesus. He was the first disciple Jesus called, and he was responsible for bringing his brother, Peter, to Jesus! Though Andrew is the first disciple called, it is Peter who gets much fame while Andrew seems to forever stay in the background. Peter is credited with great things while Andrew's accomplishments are hardly ever mentioned! Without Andrew bringing Peter to Jesus, Peter might not have become a disciple! It is the "Andrews" of this world that are the backbone of the church!

A pastor of a small rural church labored consistently for many years without obvious growth and became discouraged at times. It was only years later that he received knowledge that one of the young men who came to faith in Christ under his ministry was Charles Haddon Spurgeon. He was used by God to bring many into relationship with Christ.

For God's work to go forward there must be many "Andrews" around! God puts a premium on those who are servants! When we are first introduced to Andrew, we find him a student of John the Baptist! Already Andrew is a follower of John the Baptist. It was John the Baptist who pointed out Jesus to Andrew and told him that Jesus was the Lamb of God who had been promised to take away sin! Then, Andrew moves to the next step in his search for God ... he leaves John and begins to follow Jesus! While Andrew was learning about God from John, Peter was still fishing! While Andrew had searched for answers, Peter had searched for fish! Once Andrew has the answer he goes and seeks out his brother Peter to share the good news!

Having proved himself a good follower made him one of Jesus' first choices to be a disciple – good followers make good leaders! One quality of a good follower is devotion. Andrew was not wishy-washy. When following John he did so completely; when Jesus was pointed out, he left John and followed Jesus with the same kind of steadfast devotion. Jesus must have been moved by his example of commitment, for when Andrew knew the truth, he moved on it!

Rather than glory in the fact that Andrew was one of the first men Jesus called, and perhaps reminding his brother and the others of this later, Andrew seems happy to just be on board with the other disciples. Position didn't matter with him! The very first thing he does is go find his brother in order to share the joy of his discovery and call! Andrew as a brother sure was different than the pair of brothers we are first introduced to in the Bible, Cain and Abel! Abel's favor by God provoked an angry jealousy in Cain, who then killed his brother Abel! How unlike them Andrew and Peter were. Andrew's favor by Jesus inspires him to go and find his brother to share it! Peter was the first thing Andrew thought of, not himself! Andrew's desire to put Peter first rather than bask in the limelight of being one of the first disciples chosen shows the unselfish nature he possessed!

In this regard Andrew really becomes the very first missionary in the New Testament; he is the first to go for Jesus and make disciples! He could have thought to himself, "Well, if I get Peter to join, he had better know I was here first. Jesus picked me first!" Later, however, when Peter emerges as one of the three inner-circle disciples, which Andrew does not achieve, Andrew is never shown to be jealous or upset. All Andrew cared about was serving no matter the prestige he received – what a great leader he was, what a great heart! His selfless, serving attitude reflected the greatness of character that honors God even when it never makes a person a household name!

Our next clear glimpse of Andrew comes at a very famous event, Jesus feeding the 5,000! Jesus had preached quite long (and He was perfect!) and the people had traveled a great distance over rough territory ... the hour was late! Jesus decided to feed the entire crowd and so asked Philip a question that Philip had a ready answer to ... "IMPOSSIBLE!" Jesus asks Philip: "Where can we buy bread for all these people?" It seems Philip and Andrew had become friends. (They are together in the next story, too.) Philip, the practical one in the group, gives the practical answer, "EIGHT MONTHS' WAGES WOULD NOT BUY ENOUGH BREAD FOR EACH ONE TO HAVE A BITE!" (John 6:7)

In other words, it was simply IMPOSSIBLE! At this

point Andrew jumps into the picture doing what he had done before – FINDING SOMEONE TO BRING TO JESUS! In this case Andrew finds a small boy with a basket lunch! Andrew finds a partial solution but recognizes the inadequacy of such a discovery by saying, "But how far will this go among so many?" (John 6:9b) At least Andrew had enough faith to look for an answer, although he had found a very inadequate solution! The poor little boy, everyone talking about taking his whole lunch! Had anyone asked him if it was o.k.? Perhaps the real hero in this story was the little boy! He evidently was the only one who doesn't protest. With childlike faith he just gave what he had while believing Jesus could make it be enough! Again, Andrew finds the boy, but it really is the boy that emerges as the hero, not Andrew! Once again Andrew is the disciple in the background acting as the middleman.

Andrew was used to find the solution, although he couldn't yet see how it was going to work! Philip offered no solution, but Andrew, in bringing the boy to Jesus, offered a small beginning that would soon prove to be enough in the hands of the Master. It took an "Andrew," a faithful servant who was always looking to bring to Jesus something or someone, to effect the change needed in this desperate situation! Then Jesus used what Andrew brought! Jesus has the people sit while He takes the boy's five loaves and two fish and blesses them, and then He asks His disciples to begin passing out the food, thus serving the people! There is a good point here: Jesus asks His board members to give out the little they had taken in and believe that if used for ministry, it would be multiplied to meet the entire need! (A good lesson for church boards and pastors today still! There will always be "Philips" who will say, "But we don't have it." And there will hopefully be "Andrews" who will say, "We have something, and it may be small, but...")

Not only was there enough, but there were also leftovers! And Jesus commanded His disciples to pick up the excess so that nothing was wasted! Ironically, the leftovers were exactly twelve basketfuls; does that number ring a bell? Jesus wanted each disciple to carry a reminder the next day of God's supply. The twelve baskets gave each disciple a visual (and likely heavy!) reminder of what God can do when someone like Andrew is willing to bring a little boy and witness what Jesus can do with a gift given in faith! Thank God Andrew found a boy with something and brought him to Jesus! Andrew sought out an answer, even if it seemed very inadequate at first!

A Prayer:

God give us men and women like Andrew who, when faced with the impossible, at least look for a solution rather than complain like Philip that there is no possible way!

Real faith finds expression, even if only in a small way! Faith not only believes – it acts!

John 12:20-22 tells us: "Now there were some Greeks among those who went up to worship at the festival. They came to Philip, who was from Bethsaida in Galilee, with a request. 'Sir,' they said, 'we would like to see Jesus.' Philip went to tell Andrew; Andrew and Philip in turn told Jesus."

Here we find Andrew and Philip at the end of Jesus' earthly ministry. Philip still seems to be Philip the practical one. Several Greek worshippers of God had requested to see Jesus, and Philip seemed unsure of what to do, since after all, these are not Jewish men. So he goes and talks to Andrew about the issue ... what should he do? (They probably approached Philip because "Philip" was a Greek name, and they were Greeks. Still, a thorny issue arose. These were Greeks who had rejected Judaism.) Should they be allowed to see the busy Jesus? Andrew would know what to do!

Andrew is still Andrew! He doesn't go to Jesus with the problem, at least not by himself – he brings Philip to Jesus with the issue! Here is Andrew doing again what he always does best – bringing people to Jesus! Andrew is sensitive to not reject outright the Greeks who wanted to see Jesus! Judging by the statement Jesus gives in 12:32, "And I, when I am lifted up from the earth, will draw all people to myself," the Gentile Greeks were already present – thus Andrew must have gone and gotten these Greeks and brought them to Jesus, exactly what we would expect from an Andrew! Andrew's ministry was always one of being in the gap, going for Jesus, and bringing people to Him! He doesn't fill the role that his more famous brother Peter did – that of a great teacher and leader. He just was a people person bringing others to Jesus! He shows no jealously at any point toward his more famous brother, though overshadowed by him, even though Peter came in after him!

What a great disciple Andrew was! Jesus called a "people person" before calling great teachers! Andrew was the kind of follower that was obedient even when he couldn't always understand what was going on; he continued to be faithful! This is a mark of great leaders, faithful even when stumped!

Guess what the name "ANDREW" means? When translated literally it means, "MANLY!" Andrew is no wimp! A guy who knows how to bring people to Jesus is no sissy, he is a man! In Proverbs it says, "The man who wins souls is wise!" Andrew is the unrecognized strength of the disciples! While not always out in front, he is the cement of the group, bridging the gap between Jesus and others!

A Prayer:

God give us "ANDREWS" in the church! We need those who don't see how impossible something is but can find a way to Jesus! Somebody has to go and beat a path to the Lord. If there is no path then they will make one! God give us "Andrews" who are looking to bring people to Jesus!

It takes a real man (or woman!) to serve Christ. Sissies can't make it! God make us to be like Andrew who was always willing to bring someone to Jesus, no matter what was going on at the moment! Andrew certainly wasn't the most popular disciple of Jesus, nor the most up front as a teacher. He didn't make the inner circle with Jesus like Peter did – but there would have been no Peter without Andrew – and it was Andrew who popped up again and again solving the problem of people who needed Jesus by simply bringing them to Him! THE CHURCH NEEDS "ANDREWS!" Will you be one?

Andrew's gift was that of a "middleman" or "second fiddle." He was the helper in the group, acting as a bridge. He connected his brother, Peter, to Jesus, and then stayed in the backdrop while Peter grew more prominent. He brought people to Jesus; while the others taught by word, he taught by example. The church still needs middlemen — those who can speak by action and not just words, those who know how to lead others to Jesus Christ!

Are you an Andrew?

James

If there is one thing that can keep a Christian from being a productive saint, it is the beast we call a "TEMPER." A quick temper has ruined more saints than many other sins, hence the many warnings in the Bible about the wrong use of "anger" such as "fighting" or "murmuring against one another" – or "disputing." Anger that expresses itself in ungodly ways only creates more pain for those who unleash it as well as for those who are its object!

James was the "lightning bolt" of the group! However, his quick temper and sense of superiority were tamed by God's Spirit, and the James who learned to be controlled by the Spirit of God instead of his own quick temper became one of the great leaders in the early church!

The Bible teaches us that God desires to tame our quick-tempered spirit if we have a tendency toward one. The fire of the "lightning-bolt spirit" once channeled can be quite powerful, but if it strikes anywhere at a moment's notice, it leaves great scars and damage!

We can deduce some interesting things about "James the lightning bolt" – there is enough information to get a likely picture of his home life and upbringing. His father's name was Zebedee; his mother's name was Salome. Tradition says his mother was the sister of the Virgin Mary, thus making Jesus and James cousins. His family must have been rich (or at least well off) since it is mentioned that his father had a boat with servants on it – perhaps he even had several boats. Only the wealthier businessmen could afford servants on their boats – so we know he came from a family of wealth. It is also quite possible that Zebedee had a house in Jerusalem since John 18:15 clearly indicates that John was known by the high priest Caiaphas in more than just a casual way. His father's wealth may have meant a high social standing in this area and thus a friendship with Caiaphas. His brother, John, was able to go right in with Jesus to Caiaphas – no other disciple did this.

So, James probably came from a wealthy, influential family that was well connected to the religious authorities. With his father having servants he was likely used to the good life, being waited on and getting his way frequently. With his family being friends with the high priest he was accustomed to having special privileges. Perhaps this helps explain later the incident of asking Jesus to give him and his brother, John, the privilege of being seated on Jesus' right and left side when the kingdom was well established; after all, they were used to being next to the high priest already! James and his brother may have been accustomed to getting what they wanted, maybe even somewhat spoiled! This might help explain the "fiery" nature they often expressed. They were familiar with getting their own way, and if they didn't, perhaps they threw a fit! They may have come from a family that could throw their weight around in high circles, thus they were used to telling others what to do. They were probably in charge of the servants that worked for their father so they knew how to give orders. The successful business environment and prosperity they had grown up with and that they had experienced had also bred in them a hard-working ethic. They were hard-driving, hard-working men.

We are introduced to them as disciples called by Jesus, and interestingly enough it is JESUS who gives them the name BOANERGES, which translated, means "Sons of Thunder"! Since Jesus is the one that gives them this name, it is a sure bet that their personality trait in this area was the strongest when they first joined the disciples! Their reputation for having a quick temper was obvious to everyone, and so Jesus gives them their nickname! You can only guess how the family took these two boys dropping out of the family business to follow Jesus. Perhaps it resulted in some "fiery" exchanges between the parents and boys!

How well do you think a couple of well-connected rich kids coped with joining a poor itinerant preacher that constantly demanded from them UNSELFISHNESS and SERVANTHOOD!? They must have had plenty of arguments with Pastor

Jesus about how He did things and their position in the group! They must have had their feathers ruffled many times in the beginning when Jesus expected them to serve others rather than have servants take care of them! When asked to do menial tasks, they must have griped around some and thrown some temper tantrums, especially if Jesus didn't do it their way!

Jesus would not have given them a name that didn't apply! Men like this often miss the bigger picture and so get mad at the wrong things. They are so focused on seeing things only from their own context that they can't see anything else.

It must have been hard for them to be a part of an organization that rarely if ever had money or savings, always just barely paying the bills with little or nothing left over. It must have been hard for them to see Jesus make commitments to do things that would cost more than they had on hand! How many times they must have questioned Jesus' leadership skills and choices to minister to people who were considered the "scum" of society. They must have thought that Jesus would do better to court the high society folks, the ones who had power and influence! They must have questioned the game plan of Jesus, if they even thought He had one! They might have thought, "Why are we just wandering around preaching parables? What's the goal here, where are we going, where should we be going?" etc.

Mark 10:35-45 (NIV)

35 Then James and John, the sons of Zebedee, came to him. "Teacher," they said, "we want you to do for us whatever we ask."

36 "What do you want me to do for you?" he asked.

37 They replied, "Let one of us sit at your right and the other at your left in your glory."

38 "You don't know what you are asking," Jesus said. "Can you drink the cup I drink or be baptized with the baptism I am baptized with?"

39 "We can," they answered.

Jesus said to them, "You will drink the cup I drink and be baptized with the baptism I am baptized with, 40 but to sit at my right or left is not for me to grant. These places belong to those for whom they have been prepared."

⁴¹ When the ten heard about this, they became indignant with James and John. ⁴² Jesus called them together and said, "You know that those who are regarded as rulers of the Gentiles lord it over them, and their high officials exercise authority over them. ⁴³ Not so with you. Instead, whoever wants to become great among you must be your servant, ⁴⁴ and whoever wants to be first must be slave of all. ⁴⁵ For even the Son of Man did not come to be served, but to serve, and to give his life as a ransom for many."

Here we may have a classic example demonstrating James and his brother's disposition and spoiled background. They are asking Jesus for the seats of honor and prestige – the right and left seats when Jesus begins His rule! Matthew's account of this story tells us that their mother, Salome, put them up to this request. This may tell us where they got their lightning-bolt personality from! Notice their request, "Teacher, we want you to do for us whatever we ask." (Does this sound like a couple of spoiled rich kids who are used to getting their own way and being waited on?) This statement alone speaks volumes about their personalities! These were men used to getting what they wanted, and if they didn't, you can easily guess how they might have reacted – angrily!

Not only were they demanding, a trait of hot-headed personalities, but they were also arrogant! Notice that when Jesus explained to them the sacrifice and pain that will come to those who get such a privilege, they responded to Jesus' question, "Do you think you can drink from this cup?" with a quick response, "WE CAN." They weren't really thinking about what "CUP" Jesus meant; the only things going through their minds were "privilege" and "power" – not "persecution"!

As expected, their arrogance ruffled the feathers of the other ten disciples. Read John 10:4. Soon a real fight broke out between James and John and the other ten disciples! This is the other side of a quick temper; it alienates other people by appearing to be superior. "Sons of thunder" often have low tolerance for those they perceive less aggressive!

They are pushy and arrogant, which only drives others even further away!

It is noteworthy that Jesus quickly takes charge of the group to heal the developing rift. You can almost hear them: "Look, it's me (James) and my brother, John, who are in the inner circle of Jesus' confidants!" The response comes back, "If you think you should have those seats, then how come we do all work around here?" James replies, "Because WE know how to run a business better than you."

Jesus' response to the twelve at this point was to explain to them real power in the kingdom – SERVANTHOOD! Jesus' appeal was based on His own example, for even He came to serve and not to be served! Thus He addresses James' and John's arrogance and superiority, and also teaches them all how position and power is achieved in HIS kingdom! The real place of honor awaits those who set themselves aside and seek to help others first! This had to be humbling to James and John! You can imagine that they might have been highly critical of the other disciples at times, certainly another symptom of a "son of thunder" personality!

It is not critics that will build the kingdom of

God. It is construction workers!

Even as we near the end of Jesus' earthly ministry, after years of being with Jesus, James and his brother, John, reveal that their "sons of thunder" personalities are still present! Jesus was in a hurry to get back to Jerusalem in time for the Feast of Tabernacles, so they were going to pass through Samaria – the land of people that hated the Jews. The Samaritans took great pleasure in denying food and housing to Jews traveling to Jerusalem since they felt that Mount Gerizim was the proper place to worship God and not Jerusalem! Remember the argument of the Samaritan woman with Jesus in John 4? The hostility was fueled by each side racially hating the other!

Jesus sent the "boys" into the Samaritan village to make preparations, and of course they were badly treated and rejected, something that "hot heads" don't take well! Their reaction is typical of a "son of thunder" personality! "Lord, do you want us to call fire down from heaven to destroy them?" They weren't going to put up with people who treated them like this! They wrongly assumed that this would make Jesus just as angry as it made them. They may have thought, "Jesus won't put up with this either!"

Jesus' response to them is quite different from what they thought it would be. Jesus rebukes them instead of the enemy! And then Jesus instructs them to take another way home rather than stand and fight! They might have thought this was the wimpy way out. "How could Jesus do this?" Jesus could see past their immediate anger. He knew there were much bigger issues to fight than just this local situation! James and John wanted to wipe the Samaritan opposition off the face of the earth! They couldn't see past their immediate feelings. They had no control over their expressions of anger!

It is amazing what people will fight over and how we can fail to see the bigger picture in times of anger – "sons of thunder" get lost sometimes in their immediate feelings and just react without thinking of consequences or the bigger picture!

Notice that in the passage just before this one, John (and perhaps James, too) had attempted to stop a man from driving demons out of others in Jesus' name simply because the man didn't belong to the elite group of disciples. Jesus corrects John for his arrogant attitude!

They were still learning to channel their fire correctly, yet we must also note that "sons of thunder" are not discarded by the Lord. Jesus had in His inner circle of three disciples two "sons of thunder"! Obviously, there is something about this kind of person Christ sees with great potential! Fire can be tremendously destructive or tremendously constructive. The secret is control! Once brought under the control of the Spirit after Pentecost, James and John emerge as great leaders of the church. Once their "thunder" was guided, it gave power to the work of God. Jesus saw this and knew that once this energy was properly brought under control, they would be powerhouses for Christ! Fortunately, Jesus sees beyond just what we are right now and sees what we can be in Him! Some of the great powerhouses for God have been men with "sons of thunder" personalities, although usually their ministries don't work well until they come under the control of the Spirit of God! What a "son of thunder" needs to do is to take notice of where he is heading without that control and make a quick change in the right direction.

History records the successful transformation of these two "sons of thunder." These are the kinds of saints that once they are brought under the control of the Spirit become some of the most dedicated Christians whose commitment and perseverance is envied by others! In fact, when Herod Agrippa in Acts 12:1-2 wanted to scare the church into breaking up, he took James and put him to the sword in hopes that James' death might frighten the other less committed disciples – this happened in A.D. 44. (Agrippa died shortly thereafter so it had to be before this date.) James thus served God about 17 years. He was the second recorded martyr, coming after Stephen's death, but he was the first apostle murdered for his faith! This probably proved his leadership in the early church, the very reason Agrippa picked him out to kill first; kill the leader and you scatter the flock. In Acts 12 the second man seized by Agrippa was Peter, but God delivered Peter from his attempted execution! James died as an example of leadership, control, strength; an example of one of God's finest saints!

Being a "son of thunder" doesn't mean the end of all things; it just means you need control. God needs "sons of thunder" and so does the church! It is best, however, when your thunder is under His control!

James the "lightning bolt" was the typical "good news-bad news" person. He was great in drive; a fire drove him to deep commitment and action. The bad news was the quick trigger he showed for anger, which damaged relationships at times. Once God's Spirit channeled this "fire," James became one of the great leaders of the early church. He died by the sword in A.D. 44, the second martyr of faith! (Acts 12:1-2)

If you are a "son of thunder," is your anger under the control of God's Spirit?

Philip

Philip would have made a great American!! He loved practical things. WE love practical things. It is the practical people that drive our market system – and Philip was the practical one of the twelve disciples. Practical people are the ones that figure out how to get things done. We even have a saying about this, "Necessity is the mother of invention."

There are people who by their nature are always practical! There was a Martha among the women who followed Jesus; she was the practical one in the group of women that followed Jesus. There was Philip among the disciples; he was the practical one among the men!

Practicality rules the planet. Take for instance the following:

- In Tokyo there are paid muscle men with white gloves who do nothing except push people into commuter trains so they can carry as many people as possible!

- Exchanging "money" became more practical than bartering large objects back and forth, hence the development of the paper currency system.

- Indoor plumbing and bathrooms were created to serve the practical need of not having to travel outdoors to deal with basic needs!

- Cars, telephones, refrigerators, etc. all exist to serve "practical" needs.

The "practical" saint is often hardworking, faithful, and gets things done – but often they struggle with faith! God, however, has a great love for those who are "practical" – they are valued followers of Christ!

Philip was a practical man. His name means "lover of horses" and he was from Bethsaida – a fishing town – as were Andrew and Peter. These men were practical by nature; fishing was an occupation that by nature made you practical! When Philip responded to the call to be one of Jesus' followers, he came as he was, a very practical man!

Notice that Philip refers to Jesus as "Jesus of Nazareth, the son of Joseph" instead of the "Son of God"! Philip tended to see the natural before the supernatural. This becomes even more evident as we look at other passages! This was good when getting routine business done but a drawback when faith was required to do something! "Faith" is not something that just forces itself into our lives when we get saved. We must learn to "exercise" it and learn to practice it!

When Philip goes and gets his friend Nathaniel to also follow Jesus, Nathaniel responds by saying, "Can anything good come from Nazareth?" To which his practical friend Philip says, "COME AND SEE!" This was the creed by which Philip lived: SEEING IS BELIEVING! For Philip the answer came in the form of SEEING! He was a man who needed proof!

We find Philip near the end of three years with Jesus, still the practical man in need of learning to live by faith! Jesus just finished telling his disciples, "I am the way and the truth and the life. No one comes to the Father except through me. If you really knew me, you would know my Father as well. From now on, you do know him AND HAVE SEEN HIM." Philip's response to this statement by Jesus reveals the practical man he still is, and the man who was still much in need of learning what "faith" is! Philip's response ironically was: "Lord, SHOW US the Father and that will be enough for us." Notice how Philip assumes that he speaks for all. Notice, too, how Philip relies upon the "real" when he says, "Show us ..."

Philip's life had depended on the visual, what he could see, touch, taste, hear, and smell – he is having a hard time getting a handle on faith like many of us! This is so much like people today: "If only I saw a miracle, I would believe, too!" The trouble with Philip is that he keeps looking at the wrong thing all the time. This can be a painful process. His focus should have been on the spiritual world which at times is not seen through "practical eyes."

Those that look only at the physical realm will

miss out on a lot of great spiritual realities! This was Philip's problem. His focus was always on the physical realm and this held him back from great spiritual insights! Jesus thus explains to him that by seeing Jesus he had already seen the FATHER – they are the same in essence! Notice the sense of Jesus' frustration at Philip's lack of insight: "Don't you know me, Philip, even after I have been among you such a long time?" (14:9) Jesus then adds for "Philip the practical" these words, "... or at least believe on the EVIDENCE of the miracles themselves" (14:11b). Jesus tries appealing to Philip's nature at this point, "Look at the empirical EVIDENCES." Yet, Jesus does not reject Philip. He loves this practical man, and once Philip gets baptized with the Holy Spirit, his spiritual senses will kick in better!

Possibly another insight into Philip's practical side may be found in Matthew 8:21. Here a disciple that is unnamed asks Jesus to first "let me bury my father" and then he would come follow Jesus. Tradition attributes this statement to Philip – a very practical request!

Philip's faith was small ("Exiguous" – literally

"Small, scant, little"). Jesus is about to do a great miracle, to meet the needs of thousands of hungry people! First, however, Philip is targeted for a faith test. (Who better to test than the most practical man in the group – Philip!) Jesus asks, "Philip, where shall we buy bread for these people to eat?"

Philip, true to his nature, thinks on the practical level first. "Lord, eight months' wages would not buy enough bread for each one to have a bite!" (6:7) Philip has the bottom line already spelled out – "It would take huge sums of money and we haven't got any, therefore it is impossible!" Philip was thinking practically and in real terms! What Philip was forgetting, however, was who Jesus was!

Philip forgot or ignored the power of God through Jesus, that anything was possible to them that believe! Philip had a hard time seeing beyond what his natural eyes saw! If only he could see not only what his natural eyes saw but what his spiritual eyes could see! "Faith is the substance of things hoped for, the evidence of things not seen!" (Hebrews 11:1)

Jesus, however, does not kick Philip out of the discipleship group. Jesus even makes sure that Philip gets one of the twelve leftover baskets, real physical evidence of Jesus' spiritual power and authority! For Philip's baby faith, Jesus does reach him at the level he is presently at! Later, Jesus will expect more mature faith with less physical evidence! Jesus meets us where we are – and moves us on!

This tiny faith would grow, but for now Jesus challenges Philip directly as he continues to love him and nurture him! The day would come when Philip, however, would see with spiritual eyes! Indeed, he did after Pentecost. He is later martyred for his faith in Christ, and he stands his ground, rooted in faith and trusting God that the spiritual realm is real and greater than the physical realm!

Perhaps one of the secrets to Philip's growth comes from the fact that he is paired with another hometown boy with a greater ability to see faith! Andrew and Philip appear together in several places. It was Andrew who helped Philip out in the feeding of the 5,000. It was Andrew who helped steer Philip in the right direction. It took a friend like Andrew who was just as practical but also understood how to see the spiritual realm a little better to guide Philip to greater faith!

Philip is a Greek name, and he had strong Greek connections, so it is quite understandable that these Greeks who were curious about Jesus came to him first! Interestingly, like Philip, these Greeks seem preoccupied with "SEEING" with natural sight, for they asked, "We would like to SEE Jesus." (The idea being to interview Jesus or interrogate him for answers.) Philip seems unsure of how to handle the situation, or else why didn't he just tell them about Jesus? He goes first to Andrew who seemed to know better just what to do. Philip knew Jesus came for the Jews. These were Greek Gentiles, so he must have questioned, should they be allowed to interview Jesus?

Andrew spiritually understands the nature of Christ's love, that it is for all, so he takes Philip with him to Jesus. It seems to have taken Philip twice as long to respond spiritually because his practical side sometimes blocked his spiritual insights. Yet, Jesus is quite patient with Philip (even though at times He appears equally frustrated with this disciple).

Both Jesus and Andrew understood Philip. They loved him as he was, and they helped him grow! Practical people can sometimes be frustrating; they are the first to see problems with getting something done for Christ. They are the first to miss the "vision" thing. How do we deal with them? First, you appreciate their practicality; at times this is a great gift and not just a problem! Second, you love them! This is the way they are, down to earth, seeing the real world! Third, you challenge them to grow and to see beyond just the physical senses. Fourth, be patient with them – God loves them greatly and has called them just like He did you! If you are the "practical" saint – get a friend who sees by faith better than you do and learn from them! The best solution to being able to SEE in the spiritual realm is to be IN THE SPIRIT!

Jesus stayed Philip's friend and Andrew helped him a great deal, also! Practical people need friends to help them see beyond the physical realm. Criticizing them is not the right approach. Love is better! Jesus called all kinds of different people to follow Him, and He loved and appreciated them all.

Philip had strong Greek connections; his name was a Greek name. Thus, he was deeply influenced by science and Greek philosophy and culture; the Greeks were deeply rational and practical people. He was the practical one among the disciples, the "show me" disciple! This created struggles with faith more than with some of the others, but he served faithfully and grew! The Lord never gave up on Philip, and He won't on you, either, if you are one of those "practical" saints!

Simon

Zeal is a powerful thing; it has driven people to do things that are extraordinary! However, zeal can be either good or bad. It can drive people to do heroic things, and it can drive fanatics and terrorists to do evil things! The world has always had its zealots, both good and bad. It is good to be a zealot for Jesus as long as we understand the dynamics of being "zealous" for the Lord. Zeal must not be blind or without love for the right things or guided without godly wisdom.

Those who came to North America after it was discovered were all very zealous people, many for religious freedom; but for some, their zeal was to make real fortunes! Some looked for the fountain of youth in Florida; others looked for land to raise a family. We admire those whose zeal was aimed for the betterment of humanity, and we loathe those who had zeal for personal gain and selfish ambition! We tend to praise those with the right kind of zeal and punish those with the wrong kind.

Some of the finest followers of Christ are those who are zealous by nature and have aimed that zeal in the right direction, toward Christ and the service of others! Jesus loved Simon the zealot! He still calls zealots! Paul had on this occasion created quite a stir, and his zeal for the Gospel had stirred up the ire of other zealous religious fanatics – the result was a riot! While being taken by some Roman soldiers, he is asked, "Aren't you the Egyptian who started a revolt and led four thousand terrorists out into the desert some time ago?" Paul was being confused with another type of zealot! Paul had been a religious zealot, but the other guy he was being confused with had been a political one! Sometimes it is hard to distinguish one zealot from another since they all usually cause quite a stir!

Simon the zealot had been a political zealot, he

had belonged to a group of Jews who believed fiercely that no foreign power had the right to exercise control over God's people, thus a slight mix of religious zeal with lots of political zeal, also! These zealots created constant strife in Israel, ironically not just for the Romans, for they also chided their fellow Jews who failed to overthrow the Roman powers among them, even to the point that they actually assassinated their own brethren whom they felt were under committed to their cause! These Jewish zealots would roam through the Jewish crowds with daggers hidden in their coats and kill fellow Jews whom they perceived to have less commitment than they felt they should have in fighting against the Romans! Perhaps Paul's earlier life of zeal of rounding up Christians to have them executed had left him open to this kind of suspicion, but like Simon the zealot, Paul's zeal had been redirected from misguided to a zeal used by the Lord!

We must always be on our guard to be sure our zeal does not become misguided. History is full of examples of those in the name of Christ becoming misguided in their zeal! The inquisitions are great examples of misguided zeal! Killing "infidels" in the name of Christ is misguided zeal! Trying to force Christian values and laws on non-Christian people can be misguided zeal today, too! We must be careful to keep our zeal for the really important things and not get sidetracked! Our zeal should primarily be for preaching the Gospel of Jesus Christ, not primarily for political agendas. Changing people's hearts and lives will bring about the greatest changes in politics. Jesus did not focus His attack on the political system of His day. He went straight to the "heart" of the matter, people!

If we are not careful, we can easily get on the zeal bandwagon to fight all kinds of political issues. Doing so is not necessarily wrong *IF* our zeal is first in getting souls saved! Simon the zealot could not have been a stranger man to call as one of Jesus' followers! Jesus made it clear on many occasions that He was not here to fight the Roman form of government or any other type. He was here to form a kingdom in the hearts and minds of His followers! This kind of kingdom could not have been further from the desires of a political zealot like Simon! Jesus constantly refrained from fighting political issues and the laws of a secular government. Instead, He concentrated on winning hearts and thus changing the focus of lives from self-serving to serving others!

Did Jesus ignore the evil in society – either Jewish or Roman? NO! But His focus on them was that of the heart of the man or woman involved. Change that and then society and politics would change! Trying to get more "Christian" laws on our books won't make this a Christian nation if the people who live in it are not first Christians! Getting Christianity in the hearts of people will be the only way to turn America back to a Christian nation; this is the work of evangelism and not political activism in the name of Christianity! If we had half the zeal to save people as we do to do away with abortion and other offensive laws, we probably wouldn't have as much problem with those issues today! It is like the proverbial "getting the cart before the horse" when we try to create a more Christian approach without first developing Christians.

In Mark 17, Barabbas and the two "robbers" that were crucified with Jesus were all three "zealots" just like Simon had been! They had been arrested for insurrection and murder in an attempt to overthrow Roman rule and perhaps had advocated the killing of Jewish leaders who permitted Rome's authority over the Jewish nation! The common people who suffered under both Rome's rule and the abuse from the spiritual leaders of Israel had a kind of respect and admiration for these zealots ... this might help explain the crowd's desire to have Barabbas released instead of Jesus! The crowd may have thought of Jesus as a wimp in overthrowing Rome's harsh rule over them, and Barabbas at least had the guts to stand up against them! Barabbas certainly had zeal, although his was a malicious example. He killed people he considered weak or in agreement with Rome as well as Romans. The people admired Barabbas's zeal but ignored the hatred and murder of his heart, thus they revealed their own misguided evil hearts. It was not enough that he had zeal. They needed to ask what the result of all his zeal had wrought.

It is conceivable that "Simon the zealot" had a past not unlike Barabbas! Yet, Jesus called this young man who must have had quite a shock over Jesus' concepts of kingdom! Interestingly enough, not a single negative word is recorded about Simon anywhere in the Bible, unlike many of the other disciples! It is quite possible that Simon simply transferred his zeal in the right way, taking the message of salvation to others as the only hope for humanity. People of zeal tend to stay very focused, so one like him – once focused on the right thing – is not likely to have strayed!

Luke 6:15 is where we find the simple statement that "Simon the zealot" was part of the twelve. This is the only kind of statement made about him in the Bible; he is always referred to this way! What an education Simon the zealot received from Jesus. Almost all his ideas of "freedom" had to be relearned. His ideas of political freedom had to be set aside as secondary issues; freedom of the soul was Jesus' focus, not freedom from a political philosophy. It had to be hard for a man who was used to fighting for political freedom to change his zeal to spiritual freedom!

There had to be times when Simon the zealot struggled with confrontation – such as the time when Jesus was confronted with the issue of paying taxes to Caesar ... the zealots would have said,

"NO!" and then would have proceeded to kill Jews who did pay taxes as well as try and kill as many Roman governors as possible! Simon's reeducation process had to be a tough one. Jesus totally rejected political terrorism on any system, unless it was a clear violation of God's moral laws! The biggest war we wage is not against "flesh and blood" but against "principalities in high places and in darkness" – spiritual warfare!

Zealous unbelievers have a hard time understanding this concept of "spiritual warfare" or any spiritual dynamics and spiritual zeal. How many times had Simon the zealot watched Jesus deal with the political and religious leaders of the time, and each time Jesus focused the issue on the heart and not the political system! Jesus' zeal was focused on the human heart – the soul! Even when Jesus overturned the tables of the money changers in the temple in hot zeal, it was because the religious leaders were taking advantage of the real worshippers who had come to meet with God, not about politics! Jesus did not come to raise an army to advance a particular type of government over the nations, nor did He come to raise an army to kill unbelievers. He came to save that which was lost. The focus of His zeal was salvation for the lost; this is where our zeal must be centered, also!

What we need is not more arguments in spiritual circles on theological differences; what we need is more examples of Christlikeness and a passion or zeal to reach the lost! This is how Jesus reeducated Simon the zealot – by example as well as teaching!

It is obvious that Simon the zealot's reeducation came not just from what Jesus said but also from what he saw in Jesus! His original hope as a Jewish zealot was for any coming Messiah to strike dead every Roman ruler and every Jewish leader that supported the Roman government. Jesus as Messiah fulfilled none of this. Christ's kingdom belonged in the heart, not in the political system of His day and age! Christian laws won't change this country into a "Christian" country. Only Christians themselves can do this! Christian laws on the books won't do it, either. Only when our names are in the book of life is there hope for a true Christian nation.

The best thing we could do for America to restore true freedoms would be an evangelism campaign to win the hearts of men, women, and children to Christ! It was the spiritual backdrop of great people that made this country great and gave us the laws that formed this great nation! It was not a political system that shaped America; it was the spiritual dynamics that gave rise to the desire for freedom as is evidenced by the very first part of the BILL OF RIGHTS – dealing with religious freedom!

It is clear that Jesus did not come to put a stamp of approval on ANY political system, nor to wage war against any. He came to reach men, women, and little children, to build the kingdom of God beginning in the hearts and minds of His followers so their life choices would affect the kingdoms of this world! The church can exist in any political system, and indeed it has historically! It is true that in some political systems it is more difficult. Those countries like America that had forefathers who were spiritually inclined offered an easier opportunity to live out the Gospel, and as we turn away from God as a country, it gets harder as those freedoms are taken away. Yet, the church will continue on! Simon the zealot must have learned quickly and fully Jesus' idea of the kingdom, evidenced by the lack of any negative word of him in Scripture. This may indicate that he got the idea and transferred his zeal to the proper role, especially since he is always called the ZEALOT every time he is mentioned, even in Acts!

After Jesus' resurrection, we find Simon the zealot listed with others waiting for the Baptism of the Holy Spirit. They stayed in a constant state of prayer for many days in obedience to what Jesus had asked of them. Simon here is still called "THE ZEALOT" – an indication that his zeal had not waned, just found new direction!

The purpose of their waiting was to be filled with the Holy Spirit so a new motivation or zeal would propel them to preach the Gospel with boldness and fire! They lacked zeal and courage. Pentecost gave them this – "Power to be..." This new zeal from the Baptism of the Holy Spirit changed the world in one generation! Evangelism would not have been the same without this Holy Spirit baptism! What they didn't need was better evangelism programs – it was power or zeal!

What really motivates us to share the Gospel? The trouble with Americans and zeal is that we don't usually have zeal unless dollar signs are attached to it! What the church needs today is a fresh new zeal. We are the Laodicean church. We are rich and feel we have need of nothing, but we are in truth naked and poor. We need a fresh revival of zeal to get things moving again! A few disciples like SIMON THE ZEALOT would be healthy for the church!

Our zeal, of course, needs to be properly focused on people and their salvation; all the other things are just that, other things! We have plenty of zeal for programs, facilities, equipment, finances, etc. What we need is zeal for the right thing – salvation! The lack of verses mentioning Simon the zealot probably indicates that Jesus had little if any problems with him. His zeal, once focused in the right direction, must have made him stay on the straight and narrow path, although it did require new learning on his part!

Simon was a freedom fighter – a zealot! He wanted God's people free from an ungodly government and so he fought hard against political evil. However, when he found Jesus he found a different kind of freedom, not political but spiritual! Now he fought ungodliness in his own heart, and he zealously helped others find freedom from sin's dominion through Jesus Christ the Lord! He remained the "zealot" or freedom fighter, except now he was battling the right enemy!

Have you found real freedom yet? Are you fighting the right battles? What are you really zealous for?

Matthew

What would you do if you were very wealthy and very comfortable in life? More than likely spiritual things would not be high on your list. Normally this type of person is hard to lead to Jesus Christ; their comfort level keeps them from seeing their need of God, hence Jesus' warning about the difficulty of the rich entering the kingdom of God.

Matthew (also called "Levi") stands out as one of those rare examples of a man who had almost everything this world had to offer, including money and power, and yet, he instantly gave it all up for Jesus! He was a tax collector used to making quick change who made a quick change personally – and has given us one of the greatest books in the Bible, the Gospel of Matthew! The Bible teaches us that there is nothing in this world that compares with knowing Jesus Christ as our Lord and Savior!

Matthew was no doubt a very wealthy man. He was a tax collector for the Roman government while also being a Jew. Jewish tax collectors were hated by just about everyone except other Jewish tax collectors! They were hated by Romans because they were Jewish and hated by Jews because they took money from other Jews for an ungodly Roman government! Matthew's name before his salvation was Levi, thus he was from the tribe of the Levites. This made him even more hated by the Jews who saw his being a tax collector for the Romans while belonging to the priestly line an even greater than normal betrayal! Jewish tax collectors were so hated by their own people that they were called "leeches" and "robbers." (In the Jewish Talmud they are called "ROBBERS" and the term is equated with "SINNER"!)

The very term "publican" or "tax collector" was equated with "sinner" – they were so hated by all Jews! They were considered the "spiritual lepers" of society, impure and unclean, without hope of recovery! They were also ignored and treated as "outcasts." Like lepers, no one cared for or about them; they were often rich at the expense of others and so very lonely! Tax collectors were allowed by Roman law to charge any price they wanted for taxes as long as they didn't cause an uprising, thus they often taxed way beyond what the taxes were supposed to be for Rome, and they kept the difference for personal wealth – the real tax base was unknown by most regular citizens, so they just paid what was demanded – no one knew the difference! Tax collectors were so hated in Jewish society that they were never permitted to serve as witnesses in court or serve as a judge. They were even expelled from local synagogues, and their families were held in disgrace and in contempt by the Jewish community! They were considered beyond all hope and irredeemable! Their only friends were other outcasts like themselves, the scum of society — the rich and powerful who were only concerned about their own lives!

Up to this point Jesus had called simple men to be His disciples, men like fishermen, uneducated and of simple means. Matthew was so unlike these other guys, however. He was educated and very wealthy — and also considered scum! Jesus had lived in Capernaum for some time, thus He likely had come to know Levi (or Matthew) by paying taxes for Himself and His mother and brothers and sisters (MARK 6:3). Jews of Jesus' day made no attempt whatsoever at trying to win over tax collectors. They were considered too wicked to win since they were considered hopeless people — "robbers" ... "leeches" ... "sinners" ... "traitors" ... etc. Jesus, however, saw Matthew as a potential candidate to become a follower. No one was hopeless to Jesus.

Matthew, unlike the others, could read and write in Aramaic and Greek because of his education and wealth. It is he who has given us a treasure trove of information in his Gospel account. It is Matthew who records many of the "money" stories:

1. Like the laborers who all worked different hours, but who all got paid the same in the end!
2. The debtor who owed much money but was forgiven much, yet he did not forgive the brother who owed him little.
3. The story of paying taxes to Caesar or giving to God.
4. He alone tells us about the guards being paid to lie about Jesus' body being stolen.
5. Matthew alone tells us about Judas throwing the 30 pieces of silver back into the temple before his suicide.

It must have been something to witness the other disciples' reaction to Jesus' calling of Matthew to be a disciple! Matthew was so different from the others, yet his love for detail certainly has proved a blessing for all of us in his recorded Gospel!

How well will a "robber" do following John the Baptist?

Luke 3:12-13 (NIV)

¹² Even tax collectors came to be baptized. "Teacher," they asked, "what should we do?"
¹³ "Don't collect any more than you are required to," he told them.

By this text it is quite clear what the average tax collector was doing to their fellow Jews. They were ripping off their own brothers for personal gain by overcharging them on taxes! Still, they were also coming to John to be baptized! There were some that wanted to change; there was hope for some – they weren't all hopeless! John tells them that they must stop overcharging on taxes, to only tax what was required. Ironically, they would still be hated doing even this! John did not tell them it was wrong to collect taxes, just wrong to overtax.

Why would John or Jesus even be interested in such people like tax collectors? Why would God ever be interested in YOU or ME!? Matthew couldn't even go to synagogue or temple. He wasn't accepted anywhere except by fellow robbers – or John or Jesus!

Up to this point in Matthew's life, he had always lived by the tax collector's "GOLDEN RULE," that is: "HE THAT HAS THE GOLD – RULES!" Matthew had spent his life knowing how to get rich at other people's expense. He had to have developed a certain callous spirit towards others in order to charge more than what was supposed to be charged, especially taking advantage of widows and the poorer families of the area!

Matthew had spent his life taking from others and caring nothing about them! As long as he got what he wanted, that's all that counted! This was some candidate for being called an APOSTLE!

One day Jesus approached Matthew's tax booth and made a simple request: "Follow me!" (Luke 5:27b) What a surprise and shock this must have been to Matthew! He wasn't permitted in the synagogue, and he couldn't be a witness in court even if he was the sole witness to a crime, yet here was Jesus asking him to be a follower and to come and be a witness for Him! He certainly had to know something about Jesus as a great teacher and prophet. How could Jesus even be interested in HIM!?

Jesus offered no lectures about money, power, or status, just a simple request: "Follow me!" Nobody had ever asked Matthew before for something without an ulterior motive! What about all the wealth he had, was Jesus just interested in his money? This would have been anyone else's interest in him — but he knew something about Jesus and knew this was not Jesus' interest.

Matthew simply GETS UP AND LEAVES EVERYTHING! Instantly he follows Jesus. How different this was from the other disciples who were fishermen! If things didn't work out as disciples for the fishermen, they could always go back to fishing — and on a few occasions they actually did, but a tax collector walking away could never go back. It was a permanent decision! To walk away from all the money and the power, to know that there was no returning if you walked away, this took real REPENTANCE!

Matthew had a chance to find real meaning in life, and he was going to grab it before it got away! No one would know of him today had he continued in his old profession, but everyone knows him today as one of the twelve apostles because he changed! Matthew came to realize the treasure he was being offered by Jesus was a treasure far greater than all the wealth of this world! Like the parable of the man who had found the one great pearl, he sold all that he had to buy the one great pearl of his dreams! (Matthew 13:45-46) Receiving Jesus as his Lord was considered a huge gain and not a loss for him! Do we view receiving Christ this way?

The depth of his repentance is revealed by how he deals with his decision to follow Jesus. He neither became a secret follower nor kept his decision low key! He instead immediately went public with his commitment to Christ! He throws a dinner and invites all his crooked friends – he has something important to share with them, Jesus! He wanted his buddies to know the truth about the decision he had just made for Christ. Being a new believer didn't exempt him from evangelizing right away! We can evangelize IMMEDIATELY when we get saved. It does not require a special education. All that is required is that we share honestly and openly the confession of faith that we have made for Christ, and to turn our backs on our former way of life.

Matthew's decision was permanent and not some passing fad. He wanted his old buddies in sin to know the depth of the change in his life and to meet Jesus. This was his only concern, not what people would really think! Matthew uses his old wealth to bring others to Jesus! Since it was unlikely that the religious leaders would attempt to reach these people, Matthew felt he must!

If Matthew hadn't reached out to them, no one else would have. This is evident by the religious leaders' question: "Why do you eat and drink with tax collectors and 'sinners?'" (Luke 5:30) The function of eating and drinking with someone expressed ACCEPTANCE and FRIENDSHIP! The religious leaders would never have fellowshipped with these kinds of people, but these are precisely the kind of people Jesus came to save! It is hard to see people get saved that are self-satisfied and feel no need of anything!

It is almost laughable but really tragic that they asked Jesus how He could reach out to "SINNERS!" What in the world were these religious leaders supposed to be doing if not reaching out to sinners? What was the purpose of their faith in God? They really weren't any different from Matthew before he was saved! Matthew as a tax collector only concerned himself with his own needs and those just like him – ironically, these religious leaders were doing the same thing! The religious leaders only concerned themselves with their own needs and those who were just like them; they weren't interested in the lost or sinners! For Matthew, the only interest now was reaching out to others like himself who had lost their way, to help steer others to Jesus who alone is the answer to the heart problem of sinful man! For Matthew, he was used to making change – cash that is; now, however, he makes a "quick change" of character! How many people will be lost simply because we never ask them to follow Jesus because we think they never will or because we think they are the wrong type! Matthew's change was total and public! No price was too high to follow Jesus for Matthew! This was the best "change" he had ever made!

Matthew desired serious change, but not cash.

He wanted character! Jesus offered this wealthy, educated "reject" a chance to really be something – a disciple, to really cash in on something valuable! For Matthew, it was a "quick change" ... he literally walked away from his past and became one of Jesus' most trustworthy followers! It is never too late for "quick change." How about you?

Matthew's old name, Levi, was changed to "Matthew" – meaning: "Gift of God."

Thomas

The story is told about two boys, one an optimist and the other a pessimist. They were taken to two rooms and left there for a little while. The pessimist was taken to a room that was filled with wonderful new toys. The optimist was taken to a room that contained only a few items: a shovel for hay, a pile of horse manure, and a hay bale. After some time, the men went back to see how the boys were doing. To their surprise they found the pessimist in the room with all the toys just sitting in the corner. He hadn't even touched a one! When asked why, the boy said, "I just knew if I played with a toy, it would break, so I didn't touch anything!" Curious now about the other boy, they went to his room and to their surprise when they opened the door, they found a huge hole with dirt being pitched out at a frenzied rate! They looked down into the hole, and the boy was using the pitch fork to dig; they asked him why he was doing this, and this was his reply: "I saw the manure and the hay in here, so I figured somewhere there has to be a horse!"

The way we look at things often greatly affects our responses in life and our attitudes. In many ways it affects the quality of our life and whether we are stifled or growing. Thomas was the group pessimist ... but Jesus loved him and helped him to grow beyond his negative perspective.

The Bible teaches us that God loves us as we are, even when we tend to have a pessimistic heart. He will work in our lives to develop us into more positive saints!

Jesus had deliberately withheld going to Bethany to see Mary and Martha as His friend, Lazarus, was dying! The disciples probably perceived this as a sign that Lazarus must not be all that sick or Jesus would have certainly rushed to his side! Therefore, when Jesus told them it was now time to go to "wake him up," their perception of this was that Lazarus was o.k., that he had only been sleeping. They were probably more concerned, however, about Jesus going back to Bethany since He had created quite a stir there earlier; the authorities had tried to capture Jesus to kill him! And, going back so soon would surely put Jesus at risk for capture and death, plus any disciple caught with him would likely face the same thing! NOTICE VERSE 8! "But Rabbi," they said, "a short while ago the Jews tried to stone you, and yet you are going back there?" (John 11:8) They probably assumed that if Lazarus was "sleeping" now, that his fever had broken and he would be o.k., so why go back and risk arrest and death over a simple fever? Jesus had to be clear: "So then he told them plainly, 'Lazarus is dead.'" (11:14) Now, they must have been shocked that Jesus had delayed His going if this was the case, but Jesus explains the reason for His waiting: "And for your sake I am glad I was not there, so that you may believe. But let us go to him."

(11:15) A man dead for 4 days being raised from the dead would surely help their faith — even though they did not yet fully understand that Jesus was going to raise him from the dead. It was for their sake that Jesus had waited, and for the sake of others who would witness the power of His authority over death.

How differently each disciple reacted to the news that they were going back to a hostile area. Even in the same church family, we react differently to the same thing. I'm sure the reaction to Jesus' decision to return to a hostile environment was questioned. "Do you think this is a good idea with the hostile climate right now?" "I'm sure Mary and Martha will understand if we don't make it!" "If Lazarus is already dead, why go back and have twelve more funerals to deal with, namely us!" "I liked the guy, too, Jesus, but I know Lazarus wouldn't want us to jeopardize our lives if he could talk now."

Thomas is singled out here in his response, and it clearly shows him as a pessimist, but it also shows his commitment to Jesus! "Then Thomas (called Didymus) said to the rest of the disciples,

'Let us also go, that we may die with him.'" (11:16) Not all pessimists in the church are sloppy in their commitment to God; they may just be negative in their perspectives but deeply committed to God! Notice Thomas' response to going back when it was likely he would be arrested and tried and executed: "Let us also go, that we may die with him." (11:16b) He was fully committed to going back if that was what Jesus wanted to do, even when he thought it meant certain death! I would call that commitment! What a cheery disciple Thomas was! He is speaking to the whole group about his plan – "Let's go with Jesus and plan to die also!" You have to admire the commitment this reflects, although his attitude is one of expecting the worst – a pessimist!

Sometimes you encounter Christians like this. Every plan the church proposes will meet with disaster in their minds. They always expect the worst! It'll fail or there's not enough money or everyone will quit after it starts; no one will do the work; we tried it before and it didn't work then ... but hey, let's try even if it fails, anyway, etc. They may even volunteer to be involved after expressing their viewpoint that it won't work! They are committed complainers! There just are some people who have a hard time seeing the positive or good in anything!

Thomas was one of those disciples that assumed the worse in most situations – you will see this again after Jesus' resurrection! This probably meant he was moody and isolated himself at times. We will find this true in the last passage we study. At this time, Jesus says nothing to Thomas about correcting his response. Time will bring maturity, and later, the outpouring of the Holy Spirit will help him, also!

Jesus on this occasion is consoling His disciples, giving them promises they can bank on to encourage them! He is assuring them of the future, something uncertain for most people. He wants them to know that they will be well taken care of, that He is making plans for them to follow Him to heaven one day! How wonderful to be assured of the rich promises of God! We, as disciples of Jesus, need to know God's promises, especially when we are going through tough times! God's Word contains many promises for His children: promises of protection, help, guidance, and safety – and a glorious future! Like many Christians today, those promises did not seem to make much of an impact on the disciples. They didn't seem to catch the importance of what Jesus was saying.

Thomas' response indicates his usual pessimistic response: "Lord, we don't know where you are going, so how can we know the way?" (14:5) Thomas' first reaction to the good news of Jesus' promise to prepare a place for them and to come and get them one day was negative and cynical – his pessimist personality coming out again! Instead of joy for the promises of God, Thomas only sees problems! Jesus had already stated before Thomas' protest, "You know the way to the place where I am going." (14:4b) Thomas doesn't seem to know that Jesus meant He was going to heaven! What was Jesus' mission all about? How could Thomas not have known?

All this time with Jesus and all the talk about the kingdom of God and Jesus being the way to heaven and still Thomas poutingly states, "How can we know the way? We don't even know where you are going?" Maybe he had a bad hair day or something! Perhaps he was just in one of his usual pessimistic moods! After all, this occasion was full of anxiety, things were getting bad, Jesus had already had His last supper with them, and the pressure was on from the authorities. Thomas may have been bummed out by the way things were going – from bad to worse – so certainly nothing good was coming!

At least he was honest about how he was feeling! His negative slant blocked his comprehension about what Jesus was doing – this is often true with pessimistic saints. He couldn't see straight! Jesus explains this to His disciples, including Thomas – He is the way! The way is taken care of, Thomas; don't fret or be frustrated!

Following Jesus' resurrection when the disciples were hiding in fear, Jesus made an appearance to encourage them. Only one disciple from the eleven was missing on this first appearance. Guess who? THOMAS! He may have been alone, pouting, which seems likely after Thomas rejoins them and they share how they had seen Jesus alive! Thomas quickly states that he will not believe until he can touch Jesus himself! He refuses to accept the words of his best friends, an indication of doubt and being a pessimist! He may have been angry that Jesus made an appearance to them, though it was his own fault for not being with the other disciples!

Thomas is emphatic about not believing. He felt cheated. Jesus had died, and this was not his idea of a new kingdom. Now they were all bad guys in everyone else's eyes. Jesus supposedly appeared to everyone – except him, of course! Thomas saw only what Thomas wanted to see!! He wasn't optimistic about anything at this point and didn't believe anything he couldn't touch for himself! Some Christians are like this, too! Thomas' absence during the first appearance of Jesus may have had a lot to do with his pessimism.

Thomas was still pessimistic Thomas. "God reveals Himself to everyone else except me!!!" So, he won't be persuaded to believe until he touches Jesus and has proof firsthand! If this isn't being pessimistic, I don't know what is! This is a sad state to exist in. Pessimistic people can be miserable.

It is interesting that Jesus waits another week before showing up in Thomas' presence! Jesus didn't jump to satisfy Thomas' doubting; perhaps the Lord wanted Thomas to grow up a little bit! To constantly jump every time Thomas whined around would only have encouraged more of it! Jesus waited on purpose, just like He did after Lazarus' death! Making an important point at His next appearance was quite clearly intended by Jesus just for Thomas's sake; Jesus immediately addresses Thomas personally at His next appearance!

Jesus' wait of a week was probably meant to help Thomas work through his negative and pessimistic nature. He rejected his best friends' testimony, not a good example of friendship on Thomas' part! This waiting period must have been agony, but it was necessary for what Thomas needed in his life, to become more positive! Sometimes God uses struggles to force us to grow up, to learn something new, to teach us how to walk by faith; you can't walk by faith if it is never tested! Struggles many times are God's way of saying He loves us, not the opposite! Struggles build character. They teach us to trust God, to believe He is good even when the evidence doesn't exist at the moment to see that, etc.

Jesus must have known that an extra week of waiting would be good for Thomas! Sure enough, when Jesus comes into the room a week later, His attention immediately goes to Thomas with an invitation to go ahead and touch His body for proof! What a testimony of Jesus' patience with Thomas, yet He did make him wait a week. He knew Thomas' struggle with doubt. The invitation was clear: "...stop doubting and believe!" (20:27b)

Thomas' response is very interesting for it does not say he touched Jesus, he simply blurted out, "My Lord and My God!" (20:28) Thomas woke up quickly. He'd come around again! Like the others, the Baptism of the Holy Spirit on Pentecost seemed to have altered his negativism and pessimism. We have no other examples of Thomas being negative or pessimistic after this event. He had finally become a positive saint!

Jesus adds a final BEATITUDE HERE: "BLESSED

ARE THOSE WHO HAVE NOT SEEN AND YET HAVE BELIEVED!" The term "BLESSED" means "HAPPY" – the idea being that those who can believe without requiring proof experience a joy or happiness that is sometimes lost to those who are more pessimistic and require proof before believing! However, one can always change, just like Thomas; Jesus is always in the process of strengthening us where we are weakest! It is possible to move from being a pessimist to being an optimist. Thomas did it, and so can disciples today.

At no point did Jesus get rid of Thomas the pessimist. He just kept working with him, developing and stretching him as they went along – Jesus loves the Christian pessimist just as much as He does the Christian optimist, and so should we! He is in the business of changing us from being a pessimist to an optimist!

Thomas struggled with being a pessimist, and often it brought him pain – and certainly lots of doubt, but the Lord loved him and continued to help him grow. Like many of us, Thomas was a mix of good and bad qualities. Although negative in his perceptions, he always stayed committed to Christ. What he missed along the way as a pessimist, however, was the joy and confidence of his faith, but he did make progress and grow into a positive disciple! Therefore, there is hope for the worst pessimist among us!

Jude

If only God would listen to me! I could win the world for Jesus if God would only follow my evangelistic plan. It would go something like this:

First, we would have Jesus come down physically to this planet and get rid of all the terrorists by a hand gesture and then have Jesus rule as king over the whole planet! Second, we would have Jesus multiply all the food resources in the world so that no one goes hungry. We would broadcast on worldwide TV Jesus speaking with a single command and healing all the sick people so all the hospitals would empty out at once. No more sick people! Jesus would give gold to everyone, thus making everyone rich. Every person would miraculously receive a brand-new Cadillac. Jesus would destroy every evil political system and dictator.

This was pretty much the plan the disciples had for Jesus (except the Cadillac and TV broadcast). Jude was the realist of the group. When Jesus talked about going away and leaving them and only revealing Himself to them and not the world, Judas (not Iscariot) protested Jesus' plan, in essence saying:

"GET REAL JESUS, WHY ONLY TO US? WE ALREADY BELIEVE. HOW ABOUT ALL THOSE UNBELIEVERS? DO A GREAT MIRACLE FOR THEM SO THEY WILL BELIEVE! THIS IS NO PLAN TO BUILD YOUR KINGDOM. WE NEED TO SOMETHING DRAMATIC!"

The Bible teaches that miracles alone are not sufficient to make followers of Jesus Christ. It takes something more than that! The Bible teaches that faith and obedience to God's Word are required to be a true follower of Jesus Christ. This is the greatest reality!

Jesus shares with all His disciples in John 14:16-20 His plan for saving the world. It includes the cross and then leaving them behind while He goes back to heaven! This was not their idea of saving the world. Their ideas included some of the suggestions I mentioned in my introduction. Jesus promised them, however, that He would not leave them orphaned, that He would send them "another" (meaning: "someone just like Him") ... the Holy Spirit that would empower them and help them. Jesus does promise them that He will appear to them before He goes back to heaven, but He will NOT APPEAR to the world before He goes back. This is the issue that brought out "Judas the realist" to question Jesus' plan!

What kind of crazy plan did God devise for saving mankind? Why not just open the heavens and tell off all the sinners and make everyone get saved? For one thing, this wouldn't be love, it would be coercion! People forced this way would resent having to serve God!

Jesus' plan was so much better, to show His love by paying the price for our sins and then, in love, invite those who wish to fellowship with Him to come. This way it becomes our choice! The condition of coming is simply faith, something both rich and poor can give! His first coming was an invitation; the second coming will be to set things straight! He came to reveal Himself to those who respond by faith FIRST. Faith thus is a requirement.

This "cross" concept just didn't sit well with "Judas the realist!" It still doesn't sit well with realists today! Most people today who are "realists" have a hard time understanding the concept of salvation by the cross of Calvary; they still think science and shared wealth will solve mankind's problems. What we need, according to realists, is better education, better jobs, better politicians, and better health ... then the world will be saved.

Jesus' plan for them while He is gone is for them to obey His Word; and to help them with this, He will give them His Holy Spirit! Jesus clearly connects "loving Him" with "obeying His commands"! Their obedience to His Word would keep them close to Him. This is the fruit of love and obedience.

Judas for the most part ignored this part of what Jesus was trying to tell them. His concern was more about Jesus' plan to reveal Himself to them but not show Himself to the world later on. To Judas, Jesus' plan didn't seem very realistic. Why would people obey Jesus if they never saw Him? Judas' question was an attempt to say to Jesus, "Don't you think we should consider another more realistic program, Jesus?"

What Judas was really saying was, "Show yourself physically to the whole world with power after you come back and then everyone will follow you without question!" Jesus was appealing for people to follow Him because they believed in Him and in His Word. If they desired to follow Him, they should obey His commands.

Judas the realist just wasn't buying Jesus' plan. It didn't make sense. It just didn't seem like a realistic plan for winning the world! "Come on, Jesus, there has got to be a better way to do this!" "Be real. If you want to get the word out, show yourself to everyone!" "If you want them to follow you, show power, do miracles, be a king!"

Certainly, Judas had a better way! "Jesus, let's talk about getting you a spot on the Tonight Show. Millions will see you and become followers." "We'll make a movie; this is the way it is done today."

"We'll build beautiful buildings that will create 'awe' in people." "We'll feed the poor and heal the sick. This will get them all!"

Judas wasn't convinced Jesus' plan would work. If only believers see Him, then how will anyone ever become a believer? The realist is troubled by God's plan of salvation. Why FAITH? Wouldn't it be easier if God proved His existence? There are still those today that can't understand this requirement of the "FAITH" thing, and why God doesn't simply show up and prove Himself! When God did prove it by sending Jesus in the flesh and doing the miracles such as raising the dead and feeding the multitudes and healing the sick, the realists out there crucified Jesus rather than believe on Him! People still didn't believe even when they got the miracles!!! Today people simply rationalize miracles away if they see or hear of one! Most people would rather not think about God or the sacrifice Jesus made for them. They just ignore Christ and go about their business. Even a great sacrifice can be ignored, as existing miracles can be!

Only those who take notice of what our heavenly Father did in sending His only Son to die for us will find the joy of salvation. It is by faith that we enter into salvation. Certainly, Judas must have thought some other way would be more realistic in reaching the lost, the BIG miracles perhaps, and some other way besides just believing! Jesus had previously addressed this issue in the story of the rich man who found himself in Hell and desired Lazarus, who had gone to Paradise, to rise from the dead and go to his five brothers and warn them about the reality of Hell. If someone from the dead showed up, they would certainly believe, or so he thought! However, the reply of Abraham to the rich man lays out the same plan that Jesus later espoused, namely that the Word of God is the way in: "They have Moses and the Prophets; let them listen to them." In essence, he implies that the Scriptures contain it all!

The rich man, however, uses the same logic as Judas. His question implies this clearly: "No, father Abraham, if someone from the dead goes to them they will repent!" but Abraham says, "If they do not listen to Moses and the Prophets, they will not be convinced even if someone rises from the dead." (16:31) The idea that great miracles alone will bring people to Jesus is wrong!!!! If they saw one, they would rationalize it away if they didn't already have faith! If people ignore the Bible, they will certainly ignore miracles or they will excuse them by some rational explanation! To ignore the prophets is to ignore Jesus. He was (and is!) the greatest prophet and more! The point here is simple: REALISTICALLY, Judas "the realist" wasn't being very realistic! It is God's Word that dramatically changes those who believe it! This was Jesus' chosen method for revealing Himself in time! No miracle changes people more than God's Word!

It is not GREAT WISDOM that saves people. It is GOD'S WORD! There is no substitute for the Holy Spirit using God's Word to convict hearts and turn them toward Jesus. This is why Paul said, "For the message of the cross is foolishness to those who are perishing, but to us who are being saved it is the power of God." And, "For since in the wisdom of God the world through its wisdom did not know him, God was pleased through the foolishness of what was preached to save those who believe." (1 Corinthians 1:18, 21)

Jesus' reply to Judas the realist is the central dynamic to salvation still! "If anyone loves me, they will obey my teaching!" Being a Christian means obeying Christ's commands and teachings. His Word becomes our guide, not the wisdom of this world. It is God's Word that gives clarity to the plan of God in salvation – this is why we stress the Bible so much. It is the only plan for salvation! There are no other paths to God! You either love the Word of God or you don't. You cannot read it and be neutral. God's Word will either turn you toward God or toward hell, which is why there is such hostility towards the Bible by unbelievers.

The realist in the kingdom of God understands the importance of God's Word and the plan of salvation! For Judas the realist, the message was clear: "OBEDIENCE TO MY WORD BY FAITH IS THE WAY TO LIVE." Miracles alone will not bring people to Christ; if they don't have faith in Christ, they will simply explain the miracles away, even if they see them happen. Realistically, reaching the lost will require us to use the Word of God, by PRACTICING it and PREACHING it!

Like most realists, Judas (also called Thaddaeus) didn't understand why Jesus didn't just publicly show Himself when He was resurrected, thus proving to the world who He was – the Son of God! Jesus' answer to him is still true today: He has revealed Himself through His Word. Miracles don't make converts. Faith in Christ and obedience to God's Word do!

James the Less

Oh, how we all want to be special, popular, or famous! It was no different with most of Jesus' disciples! James and John wanted to have the right and left seats next to Jesus when He ruled the world ... Peter was always at the front grabbing attention about how strong his commitment was. Simon the Zealot wanted to conquer Rome and free the nation – to be a hero. Matthew (while he was a tax collector) wanted riches and fame from Rome. One guy however was content to just be the "ORDINARY" one in the group. His name was JAMES THE LESS or JAMES THE YOUNGER. He was called the younger or "less" because he was Matthew's younger brother.

Tradition says he, too, was a tax collector before becoming a disciple, but evidently not as famous or cutthroat as his older brother, Matthew.

Most of us dream of being something greater than just ordinary, and there will probably be a few times in your life when you will attract greater attention, but most of life will likely be filled with boring, ordinary days.

While we may have a tendency to look down upon this ordinary life of ours, it is here that much of the good of our lives actually develops. These "ordinary" times are just as valuable as the greater moments, even if others don't think so!

The great composer Irving Berlin wrote some of the greatest songs known to man, including, *God Bless America, I'm Dreaming of a White Christmas*, and others. One day when interviewed, he was asked this question: "What do you think of the many songs you've written that didn't become hits (or famous)?" Berlin's answer was instructive: "I still think they are wonderful!" To him they were just as wonderful as the well-known songs he wrote, just that nobody else thought so! This is how God looks at the famous and the not so famous saints. The great ones are great and so are the ordinary ones! God as author loves everyone He has made! Ordinary is o.k.!

God's Word teaches us that He takes great delight in the "ordinary" disciple; it is not fame God looks for in us as much as it is faithfulness! Some of his most reliable and stable followers are quite ordinary!

"James the younger," what does the Bible tell us about this disciple? – NOTHING! There are no stories about him! Nothing bad is recorded about him anywhere! He seems to be ignored in the Bible except to remind us from time to time that he was with Jesus and that he served faithfully by virtue of being one of the apostles. He was in the upper room and filled with the Spirit; he saw Jesus after the resurrection, etc. Matthew, his older brother, seems to have overshadowed him. That's why he was called the "younger."

He was practically invisible in history, but he was always faithful to serve, or the Bible would have recorded his fall as it did the others when they fell. So many of God's consistent servants are like this, quietly living out their lives in obedience to God's

Word, never grabbing the attention or headlining, just being faithful day by day. Their names may never go down in the annals of history, but they are written in the book of life!

Many times these ordinary believers minister without notice by others. How anemic the church would be if it only had the services of its leaders and those who are always out front and not the men and women like "James the less" who are the faithful servants behind the scenes faithfully serving though not always noticed.

Like Booker T. Washington in his autobiography *UP FROM SLAVERY*, where he writes how the hardest thing he endured as a slave was the flax shirts they were given to work in. These cheap shirts would cut the skin open and chafe so bad as to create sores. Only after these shirts were worn for some time did they become comfortable. His older brother who never achieved fame like he did used to take the new shirts and wear them until they were broken in so that Booker didn't have to suffer the cutting and prickly feeling of the shirts ... he did this for the love of his brother! – *Source Unknown*

Where did James acquire the GIFT TO BE

ORDINARY? The influence probably came from his mother. His mother is mentioned several times, usually with Mary, the mother of Jesus. Here she is mentioned as one of the women who followed Jesus and cared for Jesus' needs, the practical and ORDINARY stuff! In other words, his mother was a model of being ordinary and extremely practical – and faithful. These women were evidently women of means. If Matthew, his older brother, and he had been tax collectors, it is quite possible their father had been one too, and so they had become a wealthy family. Now that their wealth was turned to serving Christ in down-to-earth practical ways, the family went from social standing among the rich to becoming ordinary servants to Jesus.

James' mother was also there the day of Jesus' resurrection to help anoint Jesus' body for what she thought would be a permanent burial. His mother's concerns were again eminently practical, not to become famous! His mother was a model of behind-the-scenes ministry, of just being an ordinary servant with an extraordinary commitment!

No doubt his mother had set the focus for this family. She had taught her boys to focus on the really important stuff, the common, ordinary touch. Where our focus is directed is usually where we end up! If you focus on being some great person, you will never get down to the business of serving faithfully day by day. You'll always be looking for the moment when you can do something so great that everyone will take notice! Where is your focus?

It is not a stretch of imagination to guess that "James the younger's" record of service was impeccable; otherwise, surely the Bible would have recorded his errors as indeed it did with almost every other disciple who failed. This lack of information may be an indication that there was nothing to report that was unusual, neither great nor bad – just ordinary faithful walking; being consistent in his level of service. James was the kind of disciple that simply served as he was expected to serve. He didn't assume others would take care of the need if he didn't do it. Like his mother, he probably looked for what needed to be done and just did it.

How unlike service today in God's kingdom where others sometimes assume someone somewhere down the line will somehow take care of serving where the needs are. This quiet behind-the-scenes apostle served faithfully, though in ordinary ways most of the time ... he never reached FAME, but boy, he reached FAITHFULNESS!

In his brother Matthew's Gospel, it is recorded that "he that wishes to be GREATEST should become LEAST" or a SLAVE to others. James was good at being the "LESS"! Jesus' model was the servant. Greatness in the kingdom is not equated with greatness in the eyes of this world, or even the eyes of the church today – unless of course the church understands the biblical definition of greatness! While James has nothing recorded for us to read about, his contributions to the kingdom of God were IMMENSE! While we don't know his specific deeds, we know his name will be written on the foundation stones in heaven! We can't point out a single event he did, but his life is a testimony of great service. Tradition says he died by stoning while preaching Jesus as Lord! Great names will come and go in history, but their example and work live on.

What is the reward of the ordinary faithful servant of God? His brother Matthew's book records Jesus as saying: "Come, you who are blessed by my Father; take your inheritance, the kingdom prepared for you since the creation of the world!" (25:34) Heaven and eternal life with Christ are the promise for the faithful! Knowing this future joy and victory can have great impact on our faithfulness day by day. Even when bad things happen, we can be unshaken because we know what's coming.

When we know the future, the present circumstances cannot shake us, so be faithful no matter what!

What kind of service impresses Jesus? Look what is listed here in this same text:

> "I was hungry, and you gave me something to eat..."
> "I was thirsty, and you gave me a drink..."
> "I was a stranger and you took me in..."
> "I was in need of clothes and you clothed me."
> "I was sick and you looked after me..."
> "I was in prison, and you came to visit me."

How "UNGLORIOUS" these ministries are! This is

not the stuff of fame and greatness! These are the needs of ordinary people! Jesus' point must not be missed. Ordinary stuff is the service God is looking for, taking care of the mundane needs of others, and our faithfulness to serve in these ways! This was the man we know as James the younger or "Less"! He is not impressive for any great event recorded in the Bible, but he is listed as an apostle who served without incident until his death! This ordinary disciple is really one of the most impressive of the group! In spite of his youth and inexperience, he was faithful to serve continuously. In spite of not having a great story to tell of something big that he did, he is simply a great example of the bulk of those who will serve the Lord generation after generation! Nothing negative at all about him, JUST ORDINARY GREATNESS! Don't lose heart, Saint, if you never become famous or great in other peoples' eyes even though you serve faithfully. Someday your name and service will be proclaimed by Jesus before the entire world! Be patient and keep serving till the end of time!

The greatest work of God's kingdom is done by ordinary, unknown believers! While the world is unaware of their names, it will not be unmoved by their service! God will honor not our fame but our fidelity! Faithful, common service is the foundation of a healthy church and ministry even if you never become famous! Being "ordinary" is okay and is the hallmark of greatness in God's eyes!

Nathaniel

Nathaniel (also called "Bartholomew") means "Son of Tholmai" – possibly from a group called the "Tholmaens" who gave much attention to the study of ancient Scriptures ... Nathaniel literally means "Gift of God." He was the one guy in the group that even before becoming a disciple of Jesus was known as a good, moral, honest, and a decent man. He was the good guy in the group, much like the hard working, good moral man of today who genuinely cares about others but has never become a Christian. Such people are often rare since most humans have a sneaky side to them.

The Baltimore Orioles of 1894-96 was the best

baseball team up to that time, and also the craftiest. One of their favorite tricks was to plant a few extra balls in strategic spots in the tall outfield grass. Then any balls hit into that area where it looked like the other team might make an extra base were miraculously held to singles. They would simply pick up the planted ball near them and quickly throw it in. They finally got caught during one game when an opposing batter drove a ball to left-center field near one of the hidden balls. The left fielder picked up the hidden ball and threw it in. The center fielder, however, didn't notice his teammate had done this while he chased the real ball and thus he, too, threw in a ball. The umpire saw two balls come flying in to second base, called time and awarded the game to the other team. Their deceit was exposed. – *Source Unknown*

Nathaniel would never have played on such a team. He was a paradigm of virtue though he was not yet a follower of Jesus. Nate was an idealist, a man of high moral character and values, but he still needed Christ! Even the nicest people need the Lord Jesus Christ, and Jesus seeks out this good guy, for even the best of humanity is lost without Christ!

Nathaniel teaches us that even the finest example of humanity still needs to come to Jesus Christ to find forgiveness of their sins and receive eternal life! All the good deeds in the world cannot save you. Only Jesus can do this!

Seven of the disciples were fishermen from Galilee (mentioned in John 21). They probably knew each other prior to becoming Jesus' followers. They probably already had established friendships with each other! Notice how important it was for each of them to lead their friends to Jesus once they became followers. Andrew brings Peter to Jesus. Philip goes and finds Nathaniel and brings him to Jesus right after he became a follower. Philip was concerned over what might happen to their friendship if he followed Jesus, but his friend Nathaniel didn't. Losing his friend would have been painful to him.

Nathaniel was the kind of friend every parent would dream of having for their kids! From Jesus' own statement about Nathaniel even before he accepted Christ, we find a man who is an honest, virtuous, man – notice Jesus' appraisal of him in John 1:47: "When Jesus saw Nathanael approaching, he said of him, 'Here is a true Israelite, in whom there is nothing false.'"

He was a positive role model for others his age, a well-respected young man! He was a searcher of truth as is evidenced by Philip's statement of Jesus being the fulfillment of the ancient Scriptures, of the writings of Moses. Philip knew that Nathaniel studied a great deal. Nathaniel was a religious man, he was a good man, a man who truly wanted to know God and was anxious for the promised Messiah to come, but Nathaniel was also a lost man without Christ in his life! He was probably an idealist, as is evidenced by his comment on Jesus coming from Nazareth: "Nazareth! Can anything good come from there?" (John 1:46) In his mind, the holy Messiah wouldn't come from some ungodly and wicked city like Nazareth. It was his idealism that showed here more than prejudice! The Scriptures had spoken of Bethlehem as the birthplace of the Messiah – not Nazareth. (Philip had not mentioned Jesus' birth at Bethlehem.)

Nathaniel was a guy you could count on. His word was absolute, and he was not swayed by public opinion. Philip had done well to pick such a friend. This might also explain the lack of any negative stories recorded about Nathaniel anywhere in the Bible! Such a friend could only have been a positive influence on Philip's life and the others from Galilee. Though not a believer, he knew his Bible very well. He was a readymade Christian except he hadn't gotten saved yet!!! With all this good character, he still needed Jesus, and Jesus had his eye on Nate!

As mentioned earlier, Philip cared a great deal about their friendship. He did not want to be a follower of Jesus without sharing this with his friend, Nathaniel. As soon as Philip found Jesus as Lord, his thoughts turned to his friend's need of Jesus. Boy, what an example for Christians today! He immediately set out to find Nathaniel and share the good news with him! Interestingly enough, Philip knew exactly how to reach his friend, Nate. He knew he was a student of the Old Testament, so he tells him he has found the one that Moses and all the prophets spoke about. He identifies Jesus the Messiah to Nathaniel as "Jesus of Nazareth, the son of Joseph." Philip must not have known as much about the Scripture as Nathaniel. If so, he would have known this designation for Jesus would arouse some serious questions in Nathaniel's mind; all Philip knew was that his friend needed to know Jesus like he now did! He cared about their friendship and certainly knew that by following Jesus, this friendship could be lost if Nathaniel, too, didn't also know the Lord. Rather than just abandon the friendship, he attempted to save it by bringing his buddy to Christ! Have you cared enough about those you call friends to bring them to Jesus?

Philip's description of Jesus as the Messiah threw a well-learned man like Nathaniel for a loop! "Jesus of Nazareth?" – A city known for its vices and mixed races!! Being a man of Scripture, he knew the Messiah was to be born of pure Jewish blood and born in Bethlehem and not Nazareth, so Philip's description didn't exactly excite him! "Son of Joseph?" – Many rumors had flown around in Jewish circles concerning Joseph and Mary and the birth of Jesus. His mother was pregnant before being married – hardly the expectation for the coming Messiah's birth! This may well have raised some confusion in Nathaniel's mind. It didn't fit the idealistic thoughts he had about the Messiah's coming or what he thought he understood from Scripture. He must not have known about Jesus' birth in Bethlehem just as the Bible stated it would be, and the flight into Egypt and then back to Nazareth where Jesus grew up as a boy. Philip, however, did not argue with his friend. After all, they were friends. Instead, he insisted that Nathaniel should come with him and see Jesus for himself. Rather than fight with him or start an argument, Philip knew the best approach with a friend was to simply invite him to come and see Jesus. Jesus would take care of the questions and doubts!

This is still a great approach. Too many Christians like to argue and fight with unsaved people. Rarely does this approach win the lost – they are won when they witness the presence of Jesus and the see the Holy Spirit at work. God is better at defending Himself than we are at defending Him! Philip's method here is a wonderful example of evangelism. He does not try to answer every possible question. Instead he gets his friend to experience Jesus directly! He offers to go with him to see Jesus. He doesn't just send Nathaniel to Jesus; he goes with him. This would help Nathaniel perhaps not feel so uncomfortable. After all, a good friend wouldn't take him someplace that was bad! Their existing relationship of trust paved the way! Nathaniel's stumbling over Jesus' boyhood town and earthly family would disappear when he met Jesus!

Even as Nathaniel approaches Jesus, Jesus states, "Here is a true Israelite, in whom there is nothing false!" This is quite a statement coming from God's son! This certainly affirms the efforts that Nathaniel had spent a lifetime practicing, being a man of integrity! However, Jesus' statement caught Nathaniel off guard. In his mind was the immediate question: "How does Jesus know what I am like ... how could He possibly make such a statement without ever knowing me?" Indeed, Nathaniel comes right out and asks Jesus, "How do you know me?" (1:48) This was, after all, their first meeting. Philip had only just gotten saved himself, giving him no time to fill Jesus in on Nate. Nathaniel probably had not run around much. How could Jesus possibly know him?

Jesus' response must have sent shivers down his

spine: "I saw you while you were still under the fig tree before Philip called you!" (1:48b) "Big deal," you say – yet this flabbergasted Nathaniel! WHY? Because it revealed that Jesus was God! Very pious Jews like Nathaniel practiced a very curious habit; they would pray and study the Scriptures under a fig tree which was the symbol of Israel. Unlike the Pharisees who tried to be seen of men reading and praying, they would find secluded places under a fig tree and pray and meditate on God's Word in private ... with no one around or to anyone's knowledge! No one would have known he was there! It was very clear to Nathaniel what Jesus had just said. Only as God could Jesus have seen Nathaniel under that fig tree! Only an omniscient God could do or know this, and to have known he was there BEFORE Philip had called him!

Nathaniel's response recorded here may also indicate that Jesus shared even more than just having seen him under the tree. It may imply that perhaps Jesus had even shared with Nathaniel some of the things he may have said in his prayers privately under that tree or something along that line – this would certainly account for the dramatic reaction by Nathaniel: "Rabbi, you are the Son of God; you are the King of Israel!" This is certainly a different response than what Philip had told Nathaniel. Philip's description of Jesus was as the Son of Joseph, Jesus of Nazareth. Jesus revealed enough so that Nathaniel knew without a doubt that Jesus had to be God and not just a good guesser on the fig tree thing!

Nathaniel was face to face with GOD! His whole life he had read and prayed for the coming Messiah. He had lived his good moral life in hopes of pleasing God, and now he stood face to face with Him! His only interest now was pleasing Jesus. No amount of accomplishments and accolades from friends was adequate now, only the desire to have Jesus be pleased with him! Nathaniel now joins the ranks of the twelve disciples. He found the one that Moses and the prophets had said would come. He didn't use his good moral reputation to be a big shot; he only wished to be with Jesus and serve Him.

Jesus wanted Nathaniel to know that this confession of faith was only a beginning. It was the conclusion to all that Nathaniel had hoped for in life, but this wasn't an end of a long search, it was the beginning of a greater work for Nathaniel, hence: "You shall see greater things than that!" While Nathaniel had been overwhelmed by Jesus' omniscience, much more would be witnessed by Nathaniel as he walked with Jesus in the near future. The evidence of Jesus being the Messiah would only grow, not diminish! These were marching orders for Nathaniel. "There's work to be done." Revelation is nice, but without resolution it is only information. Finding Jesus isn't the end of our search, it is the beginning of our work. While our future is guaranteed, many lost people have none. This means a great commission to win the lost, and Nathaniel took this call seriously! We all have a great commission to fulfill if we are Jesus' disciples. It is NOT a matter of waiting for something to happen. We have a message to tell and a Messiah to bring people to!

Jesus now adds the same message to the rest of the disciples. The word "you" in verse 51 is plural, not singular – meaning this statement is given to Nathaniel and the rest of the disciples gathered with him. The meaning of the metaphor Jesus used here is simple. JESUS is the ladder to heaven, and it is

Jesus who makes the way possible. He is promising the disciples that they will all see more and more clearly the reality of Jesus as the only way to heaven. They will witness in Jesus' ministry with them a clear sense of Jesus as the way to God. This will consummate in the final days with their entrance to heaven along with all those who believe on Jesus. Again, the point here is that there is work to be done in the present! Nathaniel the good guy now becomes Nathaniel the great guy! All his good works were nothing now that he found Jesus. Now he could really be "good"!

While Nathaniel was already a good, decent, honest man, he still was lost without Jesus! Once he met Jesus, he knew that all his good works were not enough. Only the Messiah could save him and others. What do you trust in to get you into heaven? There's only one sure way in ... Jesus!

John

Neither the church nor the Christian can survive without passion! It is passion that fuels everything in society. Why do you think products are sold promising moving experiences if only you buy or use those products?

> "There ain't no power like Mountain Dew ... just Dew it!" – The commercial shows all kinds of dangerous and exciting things for a thrill and then connects it to drinking Mountain Dew, the idea being that drinking Mountain Dew is not just drinking a soft drink, it is a passionate experience!

"Princess Cruise Lines" – we all know it as the "Love Boat" – a cruise that guarantees romance and intrigue!

Cars are sold connected to such things as bathing beauties, dangerous mountain climbing, treks through the wilderness where only beasts go, etc.

Certain beers used to promise you a pool in the middle of the desert with all kinds of beautiful girls and partiers that would magically show up to share the moment with you!

An ATT commercial a couple years ago promised their lines would be so clear and cheap that family members at odds with one another would call each other and reconcile – talk about passion!

All humans are passionate. We don't first become passionate when we get saved, but we must exchange our passions – the wrong ones for the right ones!

The Bible teaches us that we must submit ourselves to God for developing the right passions or our lives can experience anything from emptiness to damage. Christians must guard against passions that hurt themselves and the body of Christ ... or others.

The disciples in these early days of ministry found themselves "REASONING" (KJV) as to which of them would be greatest! The word "argument" is literally "reasoning" ... thus meaning more than just a sudden thing. They were backing up their claims with examples, bragging on themselves as if to convince the others that they were God's gift to the church and the Lord – passionately trying to prove their point! You have to say they all were quite passionate, but this was passion that hurts the body of Christ and the believer that displays this attitude!

Imagine how this could have impacted their friendships with one another had Jesus not stepped in to correct this? How often, however, does this attitude infiltrate the church today and is left unchecked or unchallenged? What about those Christian critics that have a hard time saying anything good about the church? They only focus their perceptions on the weak areas, suggesting that if only they were in charge, things would be different! Jesus has to step in to redirect their passion and pride. Greatness has little to do with grandstanding or brilliance, but more to do with SERVICE from love for even the smallest need!

Upon hearing Jesus' explanation of being the greatest in the kingdom ... serving others for Jesus, John immediately tries to complain to Jesus about some stranger he had seen who was trying to cast out demons in Jesus' name though he hadn't joined the disciples! He seems to give away that he had failed in casting out the demon himself; his pride was hurt and his position as an "official" disciple made him angry at this other person – who may have succeeded! Perhaps his own hurt pride was at the base of this. John and the others had just come from a failure to help deliver a boy from demons and now some stranger may have succeeded where they had failed without even being a part of their close-knit group! Their wounded pride was showing, and their passion wasn't as much for Jesus as it was for their own self-elevation!

Jesus attempts to stir their passion toward

fighting real enemies and to consider ALL those who help in the kingdom as friends and co-laborers! We are not called to promote ourselves; we are called to promote Jesus! When we have to have our way, our passions are misplaced. When we have to have Jesus' way, our passions are on the mark! Arrogance is a symptom of a passionate critic who feels they are always right, while others are wrong!

These fresh recruits, however, still had much to learn about proper passions. They were still concerned about their own sense of importance and rightness! The Samaritans refused Jesus; they were passionately prejudiced against Jews going to Jerusalem! This aroused a passionate reaction in at least two disciples in the group, JAMES & JOHN, the "Sons of Thunder"! Their response: "Lord, do you want us to call fire down from heaven to destroy them?" Was their passion misplaced? YES & NO? They were certainly right about the Samaritan's prejudice being wrong! BUT their passion to prove it made their own passion just as evil ... "Let's show 'em, Lord!" We must be careful with our passions and how we channel them against a truly ungodly world; we might be right and still be wrong in how we respond! Does our response demonstrate God's passion for saving the lost, or does it seek to elevate us to show the world how right we are and how wrong they are? It is possible to be right and still be wrong!!!

We find Jesus rebuking the "sons of thunder" here; destroying a few ungodly Samaritans would hardly have been an effective evangelism campaign! Their passions needed correction. Jesus expected more from them as believers and as leaders – He still expects a lot from us today!

What a change from John's earlier scenes. Here at the end of Jesus' time with them, we find a man who has gone from "BIG MOUTH" to "BROKEN MAN"! How had this come about? John had been the one to get close to Jesus! He was one of three inner-circle disciples. He had spent more time with Jesus than most! It was John who had leaned against Jesus at the supper table, the place usually reserved for a best friend! Perhaps leaning against Jesus' chest had brought him close to Jesus' heart in both senses! Jesus had pulled John in very close; Jesus simply rubbed off on him. We tend to assimilate the passions of those we hang around.

This is why people who hang with complainers become complainers! Hang around people who love Jesus and others, and you'll become like them! You will also experience their painful consequences.

John now stands alone at the foot of the cross, the only disciple apparently close by Jesus. John is in anguish, broken. This is not a time for words or chastising the other disciples for running away. It is a time to think about Jesus, not self! Gone was the arrogance and pride, gone was the self-righteous attitude. He didn't have all the answers; his passion was a broken heart for Jesus! No criticisms were offered here, though this certainly wasn't the way John would have expected things to go. He was a different man: no railings here against the Romans, no railings here against the Jewish leaders. Different passions were at work now. He had been with Jesus too long to be a "son of thunder" by exploding.

Jesus now speaks to John, glad to see him standing by! Jesus needs a man of passion to take care of His earthly mother, and not just anybody for this special mom – He wanted the man who had stayed close to His own heart! It was John who was constantly referred to as "the disciple whom Jesus loved." Jesus needed someone who didn't think of himself, someone who had learned to put others first, who had disciplined his passions to match those of Jesus Himself! What man had stayed closer to Jesus? None other than John. He was always the closest! Peter may have been first among the disciples, but John was first to the heart of Jesus. John was the "disciple whom Jesus loved."

Jesus had come to trust the passions in John's heart. He had watched him change. John was no mere spectator in Jesus' life and ministry. He had been an active participant. This had shaped him up! Critics tend to observe and judge others, while caring Christians tend to get in there and serve and encourage others. Spiritual health comes to those participating in building the body and the kingdom, not to those who watch to find the errors!

In all of John's writings we find a great emphasis on LOVE. He is one of the most passionate writers in the New Testament, connecting ACTION to PASSION. So much so that he states here that if one claims to have a passion to love God but hates his brother, he is a LIAR! It is not enough for a Christian to be passionate; he must be passionate for the

RIGHT THINGS!

John's point is very clear. Passions must be held accountable by actions! This is the missing ingredient in the world today – the world promotes passion but without accountability or proper responses! Passion without accountability promotes pain! It also causes passion to grow into other misguided actions, leading into a deeper and deeper pit of sin! Passion held captive by accountability, however, controls our appetites and guides them into proper channels!

Today there is too much focus just on PASSION without looking at where passion can take us or what to do with it. The Bible is clear – love has a focus, and a right and wrong way to show it! We must be just as interested in the expression of passion as we are in the experience of passion!

John's final word is clear, "Whoever loves God MUST also love his brother." How many churches have a passion to experience God's presence and power? Yet these same churches may be filled with people hating each other, or not speaking to one another. They want God to fill them with passion, but they have no plan to use the passion to love one another! Churches with passion but not love are not effective!!! It is not enough to just have "experiences" ... there must be "expressions" too! John went from a "son of thunder" to a "man of love" ... expressing controlled passions that communicated the heart of Jesus. He went from a "son of thunder" with a passion for self, to a "son of love" with a Christ-driven zeal for others! Being the closest to Jesus, he soon not only heard Jesus' heartbeat but found Jesus' heart beating in him! It is impossible to get close to the "God of love" and remain arrogant, hard, angry, and uncaring. What you draw close to will determine your passion!

Judas

How many people named "Judas" do you know? More than likely NOT ONE! This name is held with such contempt that no one in their right mind would name their child "Judas" – unless of course they were not familiar with the Bible! People don't even use this name for their pet dog or cat because of the negative connotation to the name as a traitor! You're not likely to find "Judas" listed in suggested baby name books!

Probably the greatest personal tragedy in history is the story of Judas. How does a man go from being one of twelve chosen disciples, a man who could have had his name inscribed on the foundation stones in heaven, to being one of the worse sinners of all time – a man Jesus described as the "son of perdition"? Note: The word "perdition" in Greek literally means: "waste!" He was thus described by Jesus here as the "son of waste."

How can a man fall from such a height to such a low place? Something edged him toward this great loss. The shock of this story is that it may have been something as simple as materialism that was at the foundation of his tragic fall!

The greater our passion for earthly things the less our passion for heavenly things! As Jesus aptly pointed out in Matthew 6:21: "For where your treasure is, there your heart will be also." The love of silver robbed a man named Judas of his salvation – and it can still do this today! Jesus' statement in Matthew 6:24 proved all too true in Judas' case: "No one can serve two masters. Either he will hate the one and love the other, or he will be devoted to the one and despise the other. You cannot serve both God and Money."

Judas was a full partner in Jesus' ministry! He was sent out like the rest to heal the sick, preach the good news, minister to the poor and to those in prison! He laid hands on the sick and saw them recover just as much as the other eleven! He must have had the trust of all the disciples since he was elected by them to be the group treasurer, something never challenged until near the end. There were absolutely no noticeable signs that something was wrong with Judas, for at the last supper when Jesus stated that one of the twelve would betray him, not one of the disciples could figure out who that might be! It is fair to say that he did all the right things, believed all the right things, acted in all the right ways, had seen similar results in ministry even!

But it seems, however, that Judas never really was internally transformed. He merely maintained an association with the group. There was still something else holding his love more than his love for Christ. Judas may have had the image, but not the substance of a believer! How many "Christians" might this describe today? The mere attendance to church, going through the motions of worship without any significant change in values, ethics, or lifestyle from the world, is hardly the stuff of genuine Christianity.

Why did Judas fall? Because his love for silver

never changed! He did join the disciples. He looked and acted like a disciple – QUITE SUCCESSFULLY! But something like materialism gripped his heart, something that refused to be transformed. He was satisfied with just being a part of the association! Judas was likely angry because the large sum of money they could have gotten from the sale of the perfume would have made a nice little bonus for him! With his eyes on SILVER, he couldn't see his need of a SAVIOR!

While Judas was building up his earthly bank account, he was slipping into spiritual bankruptcy! While he may have accumulated wealth, he was losing his soul! Sounds reminiscent of something Jesus said about gaining the whole world but losing your soul! The love of things can undercut even the more consistent church attendee! I wonder how Judas must have felt when Jesus told some of the parables He told or some of His sayings such as this one in Matthew 6:24: "No one can serve two masters. Either he will hate the one and love the other, or he will be devoted to the one and despise the other. You cannot serve both God and Money." Or this one in Matthew 13:45-46, the "Pearl of

Great Price" story – selling everything to purchase that one pearl of ultimate value – Jesus! Or maybe this one in Mark 8:36: "What good is it for a man to gain the whole world, yet forfeit his soul?"

How often had Jesus talked about the dangers of loving things? There is a huge difference between "abundance" and "true treasures." Too many people seek just "abundance" and never find "true treasure." Judas' occasional dipping must have grown greater and greater until here at the end all he could see was his own needs. Silver had won out over the Savior! How had Judas felt when he witnessed men like Zacchaeus coming to Jesus, repenting and giving up their wealth, and paying back all the money they had taken from people through their corrupt ways? Even among the twelve, Matthew had once been a tax collector and had given up his corrupt finances to join the group – how did Judas feel around a man like Matthew while he dipped into the group's funds? Judas had seen the rich young ruler walk away sad because he loved money too much to change, a loser in the eternal hope of salvation – did this not make any impact on his soul when he witnessed these other examples, both the positive and negative ones? How could he fail to see himself and the problem of wealth that was corrupting his own soul?

It wasn't the amount of silver that corrupted Judas. There was not likely a lot in their account at any one time. This is still often true in the church today! It was Judas' love for silver that was the problem. Judas' corruption enabled him to sell Jesus for a paltry 30 pieces of silver! (This was about four month's wages for a common laborer!) How many Christians have sold out their salvation or ministry for silver? How many Christians have gradually grown more and more silver conscious and no longer sacrifice like they once were willing to do? The more we coat things with silver, the more we see only a reflection of ourselves!

Judas had lost sight of eternity and focused his main attention on the temporal. This spiritual shortsightedness would be extraordinarily costly for him eternally – eternal damnation in exchange for about three years' worth of stealing some silver as a disciple, and at the end of his career, selling God out for four months' wages for a common worker – money he never got to use anyway since he committed suicide! When we invest only in the now, our pension will be little to nothing! Only a dozen men have had the special advantages of walking with Jesus, eating with Him, having fellowship with Him every day for years ... Judas threw away some of the greatest advantages that only a few men in history would ever have the privilege to experience! If an apostle could do this, what could happen to someone like us!? It was bad enough that Judas had the "character of a sinner." This was a terrible "crime of a saint"! He was one of the apostles! Perhaps he tired of the constant struggle and was looking for "easy street"! Those who think they have found easy street, however, discover a big surprise.

Judas had Jesus washing his feet, taking care of him for years, loving him; yet in spite of all this, Jesus knew he was going to betray Him! Yet all this attention and love was spurned by Judas! Even when Jesus pointed out that one of them was a betrayer, Judas ignores this opportunity to break down and confess his sins! The reason Jesus on several occasions brought this subject up was to hopefully convict Judas' heart, meaning that there was opportunity for repentance! Each attempt, however, fails as Judas simply keeps his mind on silver! He throws away all the advantages of walking with Jesus for a common laborer's mere four months' salary at the end. How many have done this for even less? "I don't have time for God; I have to make a living, you know?" "When I get caught up, I'll do lots for the Lord. Can't now, got to get more money first." "My expenses are just so much I can't tithe, now," etc.!

Judas' growing love for silver was about to break his adherence to the group, also. Although he had remained connected to the group, even that was about to go! Weighed down by a craving for more of this world, he left the group and committed the greatest sin of mankind, to walk away from Jesus! The greatest sin is not something we do, but something we fail to do. The failure to accept Christ is the greatest sin and results in eternal loss! One who rejects Christ will "sink" to a new low! Too much gold can make anyone sink if they grasp it too much and allow it to weigh them down!

It is interesting to note that when Jesus made very clear that one of the twelve was going to betray Him, they couldn't figure out which one of them it was. Judas had been a master actor all this time. It is also interesting to note in this passage that while John was leaning on Jesus on one side, it was quite possible that it was Judas leaning on Jesus on the other side! On one side, therefore, was the disciple who loved Jesus greatly, and likely on the other was a disciple who loved jewels greatly! Even when Judas leaves, the others only think he is going out to help the poor or get provisions for them all! No more horrific statement can be found in the Bible than verse 27: "As soon as Judas took the bread, Satan entered into him." How many believers eat the bread during communion but have sold their spiritual inheritance for more of this world's goods? Can we be so hard on Judas when his sin is so common and temptation so commonplace? He "left in the dark." How true in both senses!!! (John 13:30)

Judas managed to get by for a very long time undetected, but there always comes the time for making everything known! No matter how long we get away with something, sooner or later it is revealed! How hard it is for humans, even Christians to realize this! Judas' love of silver had now come to an end. He got what he thought he wanted only to be seized upon by guilt, but not the kind of guilt that leads to seeking out Jesus' forgiveness. Instead it was guilt that led to his demise. This was not true repentance; true repentance would have turned him around. This was just sorrow. Sorrow means only being sorry for what happened, but not necessarily doing anything to change it. Judas had lost both relationships and riches, the two biggest reasons for suicides still! What would have happened if he had run to Jesus instead of men who were just as unscrupulous as he was? It was too late to get rid of the silver, but was it too late to find the Savior? Instead of seeking life, he tragically sought death! Everything done in secret is now brought to light, as it always is!

His final error was suicide! He could have chosen a different way. This ended for him any hope of recovery since he failed to repent! IT WAS ACCOUNTABILITY TIME, as it will be one day for us all! How will your account look one day? How does it look now?

What he traded was life for death! He wanted to really live it up; instead, he traded in life for death.

He wanted happiness through things; instead, he ended up with nothing and misery! He wanted things his own way; instead, no one did what he wanted! He traded one of the most privileged positions of mankind, being one of the twelve apostles, for the deepest levels of Hell! He abandoned Jesus, now to be abandoned in Hell by Jesus! Was the trade worth it? If he could talk now, BOY WOULD HE! A little thing like the LOVE OF SILVER took a man from the highest privilege to the worse punishment! What can it do to any of us? Do you find yourself saying right now, "There goes another preacher harping about money"? If so, where's your heart!?

There is a "PEARL OF GREAT PRICE" that is greater than anything this world has to offer, and His name is Jesus! Don't trade your soul for temporary things. Keep your heart on Jesus, not on jewels! Remember Matthew 6:24: "No one can serve two masters. Either he will hate the one and love the other, or he will be devoted to the one and despise the other. You cannot serve both God and Money."

Judas is one of the most tragic stories in the

Bible. How did it happen? Believe it or not, it all started and ended with a love for silver and gold. It is not money that corrupts; it is the love of money! Judas kept his eye on silver and never saw the Savior! What are you looking for to bring you happiness? Better to find Jesus than jewels!

About Tim R. Barker

Reverend Tim R. Barker is the Superintendent of the South Texas District of the Assemblies of God which is headquartered in Houston, Texas

He is a graduate of Southwestern Assemblies of God University, with a Bachelor of Science degree in General Ministries/Biblical Studies, with a minor in music. He also received a Master of Arts in Practical Theology from SAGU and received his Doctorate of Ministry Degree from West Coast Seminary.

Reverend Barker was ordained by the Assemblies of God in 1989. He began his ministry in the South Texas District in 1984 as youth & music minister and continued his ministry as Pastor, Executive Presbyter (2006 – 2009) and Executive Secretary-Treasurer (2009 – 2011) in the South Texas District, where he served until his election as the South Texas District Superintendent in 2011. By virtue of his district office, Reverend Barker is a member of the District's Executive Presbytery and the General Presbytery of the General Council of the Assemblies of God, Springfield, Missouri. He is a member of the Executive Board of Regents for Southwestern Assemblies of God University, Waxahachie, Texas and SAGU-American Indian College, Phoenix, Arizona. He is a member of the Board of Directors of Pleasant Hills Children's Home, Fairfield, Texas, as well as numerous other boards and committees.

Reverend Barker and his wife, Jill, married in 1983, have been blessed with two daughters. Jordin and her husband, Stancle Williams, who serves as the South Texas District Youth Director. Abrielle and her husband, Nolan McLaughlin are church planters of Motion Church in San Antonio. The Barkers have four grandchildren, Braylen, Emory and Landon Williams and Kingston and London McLaughlin.

His unique style of pulpit ministry and musical background challenges the body of Christ, with an appeal that reaches the generations.

A Final Word

You can find Tim on the South Texas District website at www.stxag.org, on Facebook, or at his Houston office when he's not traveling his home state ministering in the churches across the South Texas District.

He'd be thrilled to connect with you and share stories of God's faithfulness.

www.ingramcontent.com/pod-product-compliance
Lightning Source LLC
Chambersburg PA
CBHW071118090426
42736CB00012B/1944